Only Fools Gamble Twice

a novel by

Natosha Gale Lewis

Write4life Productions
Visit: www.natoshagalelewis.com

Write4life Productions
Visit:www.natoshagalelewis.com

Published by Write4life Productions
P.O. Box 12723, Wilmington, DE 19850

Second Printing, July 2003

Copyright 2002 by Natosha R. Gale (softcover)
All rights reserved under International and Pan-American
Copyrights Conventions. Published in the United States.

Gale, Natosha R.
Only Fools Gamble Twice / by Natosha R. Gale. -revised edition.
p.cm.
ISBN: 0-9723049-1-6

1. Adult-Fiction. I. Title.

Printed in the United States of America.
Without limiting the rights under copyright laws above, no part
of this publication may be reproduced, stored in or introduced
into a retrieval system, or transmitted, in any form, or b any
means (electronic, mechanical, photocopying, recording, or
otherwise), without the prior written permission of both the
copyright owner and the publisher of this book.

Disclaimer:
This is a work of fiction. Names, characters, places and
incidents are either the product of the author's imagination or are
used fictitiously, and any resemblance to actual persons, living or
dead, events, or locales is entirely coincidental.

It is not a disgrace to reach for the stars but it is a disgrace to have no stars to reach for.

--Benjamin E. Mays

Dedicated to the three women of my past, present, and future: Christine Lewis, the grandmother who watches over me. My best friend and wonderful mother, Valerie D. Lewis, I now understand a mother's love; and my beautiful little angel, Courtney Christine (Lewis) Gale. Mommy loves you more than life itself! Thanks for being such a wonderful baby.

1/TAYLOR

"All I have to say is, if you're not ready by the time I get there, I'm leaving your black and narrow behind," the irritated voice on the phone stated.

I knew when the phone rang for the third time in ten minutes it was Morgan, calling to inquire as to how long it would actually take me to get dressed and be ready to go. Morgan knows me all too well and knows that I am always fashionably late. Morgan, on the other hand, is always twenty minutes early for any event.

Morgan was on her way to my house, to pick me up for a poetry reading at Warm Daddy's, a local restaurant near South Street. My girlfriend from Philly, Tina, was reading her poetry and was really excited about reciting it for the first time in public. Her work is actually quite good. In fact, I can always expect to receive a poem in the mail for my birthday and all of the major holidays.

Each time I read Tina's poems I know that her work could and should be written for some major greeting card company. I've been trying to convince her to submit her work to a publisher or something, to no avail. Since her birthday was fast approaching in a few weeks, I decided to submit her poems to the Library of Congress, to have her work copyrighted. I don't want some wanna-be running up on her and stealing her work. She's much too talented for that to happen.

"Look girl," I said, placing my hand on my hip.

"If you leave me, I'll just catch you down there. It's not like it would be the first time you've left me. So just shut up, stop trippin', and come and get me. I'll be ready by the time you get here. Promise," I said to Morgan.

"Taylor, you're my girl, but if you're not ready, I'm out. No questions asked. I'm not tryin' to sit in the back of the restaurant, looking over everybody's damn weave. I'll be there in five minutes. Peace out!" Morgan stated, before she hung up the phone in my ear.

I thought to myself, *I'd better hurry up because knowing Morgan, she meant what she said.* Besides, after the day I had with my idiotic supervisor, then coming home to have yet another argument with my mother, I just wasn't up for the challenge of driving. What a sista needed was a nice, cold glass of wine to get her juices flowing.

Morgan and I have been friends for about four years. I still consider myself relatively new to Wilmington, Delaware, after relocating from my mother's home in South Philadelphia. I'm going to always be a true Philadelphian--home of the soft pretzels, Liberty Bell, the best cheese steaks, and the world's best basketball team.

Morgan knows practically everyone in Delaware, being an alumnus of Delaware State University. We started hanging out and soon became pretty good friends around the time of my move. We used to live on the same downtown block and would go power walking together in my never-ending quest to keep in shape. A sista's gotta keep it tight! Morgan, on the other hand, has the type of metabolism that allows her to just about eat

Only Fools Gamble Twice

anything in sight and not gain a pound. My body is pretty decent, but I'm constantly in the gym. My metabolism mandates that I eat properly and exercise regularly just to maintain. What a shame, right? Just looking at a piece of cake adds five pounds to my scale. Definitely not fair, but like I said, a sista's got to keep it tight!

Morgan and her then, live-in boyfriend, Mister (his father named him Mister because he thought that way people would always have to give him respect, even if they didn't want to), lived together in a rented two-bedroom town house. Morgan really loved Mister, but he decided out of the clear blue one day that he no longer wanted to live together and told her he would be moving out at the end of the month and much to her surprise, he really did. Just like that. No explanation, no more talks about the future and no more Morgan and Mister.

Since turning twenty-eight last October, I can't seem to find the right man. I still haven't figured out exactly what the problem seems to be--probably my psychotic upbringing, but hey, that's another story.

I'm a desktop specialist for an online medical company, single, attractive, and have no children. I know that through the power of prayer and a bit of diligence, things will eventually work themselves out. For now, I'm talking to two guys regularly. One guy name Kevin. Boyfriend, I'll give him, has a divine and muscular body. Talk about keeping it tight. In fact, I've nicknamed him Mr. Body Beautiful. He's actually turned into my unofficial personal trainer, so to speak. We went out to the Main Course, my favorite seafood restaurant in Wilmington a few

Only Fools Gamble Twice

weeks ago and he damned near had a heart attack because I ordered a steak and fried shrimp. Brotha man was trippin' about me eating red meat and fried foods. Talking about it's not good for me. Please! He can save all that drama. I ate my steak and loved it. He can eat all the rabbit food in the world while he passes me my steak sauce--Lea & Perrins of course.

I also talk to this other guy named Bruce, whom I met while out jogging one morning. He's some sort of middleweight boxer. He invited me to a few of his fights, but they were out of town and I didn't have anyone to take with me. I guess I could've taken one of my little brothers, but you know teenagers' schedule, never enough time to hang out with their older sister.

Now Bruce is definitely a little touched in the head. Fine as all hell and a killer smile. I've spoken to him a few times while out jogging, but who can really get a good conversation in when they're jogging? Surely not me. I gave him my cell phone number, but every time he leaves a message and then I get around to calling him back, he's never there. Telephone tag, you know? Maybe one day we can hook up, outside of the jogging trail. No harm, no foul. As you can see, my love life is pretty boring, huh? I guess the same story can be told for good-looking sistas across America. Same script, different cast. Sounds like a Whitney Houston song or something. Anyway!

As I slipped on my turquoise tightly knit summer dress, the doorbell rang and I knew it was Morgan. I yelled out as I carefully limped down the stairs in one sandal.

"Damn, that heifer is fast." I continued muttering under my breath as I ran down the stairs to answer the door and there was Morgan all decked out in a black-and-white Norma Kamali form-fitting dress. I'm not gay or anything like that, but girlfriend was wearing that dress. Her hair was laid too. Morgan's golden-bronze shoulder-length hair was freshly done in a doobie.

"Come on in, Miss Speed Racer. You know you're gonna kill some poor, innocent cat on the road in that damn car one day," I said as I hurried to buckle my turquoise sandals, hoping she wouldn't notice that I still wasn't ready.

"Too bad. The li'l critters better stay out of my way," Morgan said as she headed for the kitchen. "What you got good to drink? You got any Chardonnay?" she asked as she opened the refrigerator door. Sometimes Morgan can be a little rough around the edges, but I wouldn't trade her for the world.

"Girl, you know I only drink wine and, no, you can't have any because I'm all out. The strongest thing I have is apple juice."

Morgan came out of the kitchen chewing on a cold leftover chicken leg.

"Are you a little hungry, sweetie?" I asked rather sarcastically.

"See, I knew you wouldn't be ready. You're gonna be late to your own funeral," Morgan said as she checked out her slim but curvaceous frame in the mirror as she munched on the chicken.

Only Fools Gamble Twice

Finally dressed, I checked myself out besides Morgan in the mirror. I had gotten my hair done earlier and was admiring how nice my new wet n' go styled looked on me.

"What's up with the natural look? It's cute. I'm just not used to seeing you with your hair down," Morgan said as I applied my lipstick.

"I'm just trying to decide if I want to get dreads. I think they would look nice. Maybe I'll try the twisties first before I go there."

"Girl, you're always doing something with that nappy head. Come on. Your hair looks fine. Let's bounce. I wanna make sure I get a..."

Before Morgan could finish, I cut her off. "I know, I know, you wanna get a good seat. All right, let's go," I said as I turned down the touch lamp in my living room and turned on the house alarm as we headed for the door.

"What do you think about driving back to Wilmington later on and going to the Butter Cup Lounge after the poetry reading? I've been promising Carla that I'd make it to her new club, but my work has me traveling so much that I haven't made it there yet. You wanna go? I hear it's slamming on Friday nights," Morgan said as we climbed in her car.

Morgan's sorority sister Carla, and Carla's best friend, Lisa, recently opened the Butter Cup Lounge. It was one of Wilmington's only nightclubs for sistas and brothas. Although I hadn't been either to the club, I heard the food was to die for and the drinks got you flowing. Every drunk's dream, huh?

Only Fools Gamble Twice

    I'm not much for drinking. I've been going to church more often, but it's pretty hard to walk the straight and narrow. I recently became saved, but I guess I'm kinda in the backsliding stage right now, going to the club and all. I'm trying. I didn't say that I was perfect. I'm not where I want to be, but I'm making the walk slowly but surely. I ain't one for preaching to somebody, but I do attend church at least two or three times a month. I tithe and the whole nine yards, but I can't seem to shake this club scene. I think it's because, as Pastor has preached, I'm dealing with a lonely spirit. For now, I'll continue to pray on it. God is not through with me just yet."

    "Now, girl, you know I have to go to work for a few hours in the morning. It's not like I'm twenty-one anymore. I don't know if I can still hang like I used to. I remember when I went to Lincoln University, I would party until the break of dawn and then go back to my dorm, take a shower and maybe a quick nap, and get up and be in class bright eyed and bushy tailed. Not anymore though. Girl, I feel like an old lady," I said as I thought back to my days at LU and the all-night, nonstop parties.

    "Come on. We won't stay long. The poetry reading is over at eleven. We can head on back to Wilmington after it's over and you can be home and in the bed by no later than 2:30. That should give you plenty of time to get some sleep. After all, tomorrow is Saturday and you have the rest of the weekend to relax. It's not like we do this all of the time," Morgan insisted.

    I thought maybe her plans to go to the Butter Cup Lounge didn't sound so bad. I've been to the Christiana River Club several times, but not many places other than that. Besides,

Only Fools Gamble Twice

I needed to spend more time in Delaware. Since my family and all of my friends are back in Philly, I'm constantly on the road heading up there. I need to establish some roots where I actually pay taxes. You know, learn who my mayor is for a change.

"We'll see. Let's see how this poetry reading turns out. It may be boring as all hell and maybe we can leave before eleven but as long as we stay to represent my girl, then maybe we can drag her out with us," I responded.

"Now you know Tina's not going to leave her husband to go hang out with us. Jared is definitely not having that," Morgan said.

After some thought, I pictured Tina looking over at Jared and him staring forward, as if to say, *don't even think about it.* Tina's one of my best friends from Benjamin Franklin High School. We used to roll thick. You never saw one of us without the other, but now that Tina's married and she and her husband are into this Afro centric way of living, we weren't as close anymore. She tried to hook me up with one of Jared's boys, David, but I just couldn't get into his type of people. Now I'm not hating on all natural types like Jill Scott and Musiq Soul Child, but I'm just not into the incense, and Mother Earth, and I don't wish to be a part of the dirty backpack clique. David would trip about my perm, my lipstick, talking about all this getting in touch with the back to nature. Not that he smoked more herb than a little bit. I mean, stop playing, for real. I wasn't feeling his flow. But it's cool for Tina, as long as she's happy. Who am I to judge her life? We'll always be friends, just not as tight.

Only Fools Gamble Twice

As Morgan and I made our way on the thirty-minute drive to Philadelphia, we talked about work, our college days, and our sorority. We had both pledged our respective sororities when we were in college. Morgan is a member of Delta Sigma Theta, Incorporated and I'm, a member of Zeta Phi Beta, Incorporated.

Last year, Morgan and her sorority sisters invited me to join The Charmettes, Incorporated. Now don't get me wrong, I'm not one to go around joining all sorts of social organizations, but when I learned of The Charmettes, my interest was truly piqued. Morgan and The Charmettes invited me to a few of their community service projects and based on all that I had seen them do, I was pretty impressed, so I joined. The Charmettes are a non-profit sisterhood of dedicated women committed to enhancing the quality of life within the various communities served by chapters and on the national level. We feed the disadvantaged; raise money for cancer research, which is also their national project; volunteer at Delaware Hospice; and we're definitely active in the African-American community.

The Charmettes were planning our annual bowling party in two weeks and Morgan was filling me in on all the events that took place at the last meeting which I missed.

When we pulled up to Warm Daddy's, Morgan instantly pulled up to valet parking. The parking attendant, a guy who looked very familiar, approached the car slowly, as if he hadn't a care in the world. Morgan blew out a hard sigh, like she was about to lose it. Morgan is the sweetest person in the world, but get on her bad side and beware.

"Excuse me. If you don't mind, we're in a bit of a rush. You think you could move it along?" Morgan asked in an annoyed tone.

"What did you say?" the parking attendant asked in an equally annoyed tone. "Look, I'm doing the best that I can. I'm the only one on duty and I've been here all night hustling to get all of these cars parked. Not to mention that this is my only day off and I was called in to work. So you'll have to excuse me if I don't run right over to you, okay, Miss Slave Driver," the angry parking attendant yelled.

"Oh no, he didn't!" Morgan said as she turned and looked at me in disbelief.

If I knew better--and I did--Mr. Parking Attendant was about to catch it. Just then, it dawned on me from where I knew him. He was actually the guy whom I took to my prom.

"Byron?"

"Hey, Taylor! What's up? Byron exclaimed, looking surprised.

"I thought that was you. Don't mind Miss Impatient here. We're just trying to get situated before the place gets too packed," I said, leaning over Morgan's shoulder to speak to my old friend.

"Girl, you looking good. You still look the same. How's everything going?" he asked as he came around the front of the car and approached the passenger side where I was sitting.

"Who the fuck is Byron?" Morgan questioned.

"What did I tell you about that filthy mouth of yours? For your information, I went to school with him. Lay off the brother,

-10-

Only Fools Gamble Twice

why don't you?" I said through clenched teeth as I sat back in my seat.

Byron and I reminisced for a few moments before I noticed Morgan growing more and more impatient. Thankfully another car pulled up and Byron realized he had better get a move on things.

"Check this out, you and Miss Slave Driver go on in. Don't worry about paying. It's on me. Just do me a favor and park over there against the wall and give me your keys when you get out and I'll take care of it. Also, why don't you tell your friend that manners are free in life, try using them," he said as he touched my hand and slowly walked away.

"Oh no, he didn't go there. But at least his slow ass gave us free parking," Morgan said as she parked her car against the wall.

"I know you're going to hook a brother up on a good tip, right?" I asked, almost afraid to hear Morgan's answer.

"Hell no! As rude as he was to me? He's lucky I don't report his slow ass to the manager. Fuck him. I don't think so," Morgan stated irately.

"Will you knock off the damn mouth? And you know what? Don't give him a tip. I'll take care of it. You know you really ought to watch your attitude. You have too much on the ball to be so damn mean," I said angrily. Morgan is extremely outspoken, but this time she didn't say a word. I guess it wasn't the first time she heard me express myself about her evil attitude.

As soon as the car was parked, I jumped out, fished around in my purse for a ten-dollar bill and flagged Byron down.

Only Fools Gamble Twice

"Hey, sweetie. Thanks for the hook up," I said as I placed the bill in Byron's hand.

He looked down at the folded bill and said nothing. He placed the money in his pocket, grabbed my hand, and kissed it softly "Still a lady. I was always feeling you, but then you knew that already," he said, licking his lips slowly.

I knew what the licking of the lips meant. Byron and I went to our senior prom together. At the time, the guy I was going out with just wasn't acting right. Byron's girlfriend was pregnant and we decided to go to our prom together since we had known and liked each other since our freshman year in high school.

I'll never forget our date as long as I live. I was all decked out in my gold prom dress with my hair stacked in an asymmetrical bob. You couldn't tell me anything that night. I was decked from head to toe. Byron rented a car and he picked me up from my house. My mom took millions of pictures while all of our neighbors came to their doors to check us out. I felt like a superstar that night. After we took pictures at my house, we went over to Byron's house so his family could see us and take another million or so pictures.

Unbeknownst to me, Byron's pregnant girlfriend was there, giving me the old evil eye. I thought it was one of his sisters or something, but when she continued to suck her teeth and roll her eyes, it didn't take me long to get the picture. I was a mess back then--actually, I still am. Don't let me find out a woman is hating on me because that's when I'll lay it on even thicker. I began letting Ms. Thang know just who her man was

Only Fools Gamble Twice

going out with. I began laughing and just a smiling a little too much, and every chance I got I made sure I moved in a little closer to strike a pose for our pictures. I guess it didn't help that Byron's family was making so much out of me, saying over and over how pretty I was and how Byron and I made such a cute couple. I truly felt sorry for her.

Anyway, later that night, after the prom was over, Byron just knew he was going to get some, but I carefully explained to him that prom night wasn't fucking night. All of our friends were going up on City Line Avenue where all of the hotels were located and I guess Byron figured he was going to be just as lucky as all of the other guys. I knew that many of my friends were going to do all kinds of freaky and grown-up things, but that just wasn't my scene. Since I wasn't dating Byron and the prom date was just an arrangement, I didn't feel like we ought to sleep together. Besides, the brother had a pregnant girlfriend at home and I wasn't feeling that at all! I didn't need his baby mama drama.

We were in the rental car and Byron tried and tried to get into my panties before we entered the club for the after party. I refused. Byron grabbed my hand and put it between his legs and made me feel his penis. I almost slapped the crap out of him, but then I realized Byron was packing something hard in his tuxedo pants. He pulled me close and then we began kissing and then he slid his hands up my dress. Before I knew it, Byron had my dress raised around my waist and was crouched down in front of me. He started licking my knees and let me just tell you, the knees are a very sensual spot. I found that out that night. He then continued up my thighs and found my hot spot. He slowly

and methodically kissed and licked my private area as if it were a piece of cotton candy. It was the first time I had ever experienced anything like that before and it surely felt as if I was going to pass out. Just then I began shivering and moaning loudly. At the moment I was exploding, we heard these loud thumps on the window and a bright light shone through. Byron scrambled to get up, hitting his head on the roof of the car, and I placed my hands over my face. Embarrassment was the new word of the century for me.

Luckily for us, it was a female police officer and she just advised us to get a room before she walked away. I guess she wanted to make sure I wasn't getting raped or something. I felt bad for poor Byron after that because suddenly the night was over. Do not pass go. I just wanted to go straight home, humiliated and all.

"You two have a good time in there and I'll see you when you come out. Now let me get these damn cars. It never slows down around here. Hope to see you again," Byron said, as he looked me up and down and then shook his head.

Morgan extended her car keys to Byron, and to my surprise, she handed him a five-dollar bill.

"Satisfied now?" Morgan asked as she received her parking ticket stub and turned quickly to walk away.

"Yes, I am," Byron responded, beginning to smile. I threw him a quick wink and turned to catch up to Morgan. When I approached her, she threw up her hand.

"Don't say a word. Also, for the record, how are you going to tell me to watch my filthy mouth, by saying damn yourself?" Morgan asked.

"Damn is not a curse word. It's in the Bible, so it's all right," I said, grinning and cutting my eyes over to Morgan, who was cutting her eyes at me.

"Bring your ass in here and stop getting on my nerves," Morgan said as we headed for the restaurant door.

When we arrived, we provided the hostess with our names and were shown to a table toward the front of the restaurant. All that worrying and they had reserved seats anyway. As we were seated, the waiter handed us two menus. Neither Morgan nor I was really hungry, but I definitely wanted a drink.

I had an argument with my mother earlier that morning. My mom and I used to be pretty close when I was much younger. My mother was an only child and she was raised in a mentally abusive environment. Her mother always told her that she was an accident and that she never really wanted a daughter anyway.

When my mom married and had me, her oldest child and her only daughter, I think she spoiled me rotten, giving me all the love she never received from her parents. Our relationship was wonderful.

My dad died in a car accident when my brother, Tyrone and I were younger and soon after Mom was caught in a deep depression after my father's death.

It's a wonder that I made it to where I am today. I remember the days of practically raising my brother, Tyrone. Back then, your neighbors really looked out for you. We could go to my next-door neighbor's and they would feed us what little they had to offer because my mother definitely had other things on her mind. She would drink and stay gone until all hours of

Only Fools Gamble Twice

the night. I would wake up and fix my hair in pretty little ponytails, wake my brother, iron his clothes and ensure that he looked presentable before he went off to school. I was determined we would survive all of the senselessness my mother was putting us through. Surprisingly, I wasn't too upset with her because I knew her when she was a fantastic mother, but I also realized the way she was acting out was her way of dealing with the loss of her husband.

My mother, brother, and I had problems but we never knew problems the way we later experienced--until mom met Winston, her second husband. The drinking soon turned into drugs and that's when I thought my heart would literally stop at the things I saw my mother do for a hit on that glass pipe.

One time, I woke up around 2:30 A.M. to what sounded like an argument next door. I heard loud voices, like the people were in the same room with me. I put on my robe and went downstairs to investigate. Surprisingly, when I got downstairs the house was the same way that I had left it, spotless. I went to the door and it must have been the coldest night of the winter. Our next-door neighbors, who were drunks and squatters, were outside without shoes on, arguing with Winston. Suddenly one of the squatters, Kevin, saw me. He began yelling for me to get my crack-head mother out of his house. All of a sudden, my mother was practically thrown from the house with nothing more than a T-shirt on. From the waist down she was completely naked. I ran down the steps and tried to cover her up with my robe, but she ran down the street and disappeared around the corner. Winston never even went after her, he simply continued to argue with Kevin about a damn crack vial. I ran in the house

Only Fools Gamble Twice

to get a pair of shoes and a coat, but when I got around the corner, I couldn't find my mother. I didn't see her for about two days after that, and when she returned home she looked even worse than she had before.

Don't ask me how I made it through high school with honors. I received several scholarships. My top two choices for college were Spelman College and Hampton University, but I was torn between furthering my education and being there for my family. To make matters worse in my junior year of high school, my mother became pregnant with my younger brother, Malik and then she checked herself into a rehabilitation center so she could try to be healthy for the baby. She even kicked Winston out of her life, which was the best choice she's probably ever made since he was the person who had introduced her to drugs.

I was uncertain about Mom's recovery and apprehensive about leaving her with the responsibility of raising a new baby and my brother Tyrone behind, but Mom convinced me that she was doing much better and was on the road to recovery, one day at a time. I accepted a scholarship from Lincoln University so I could pursue my goals, but still stay close to home to be there for my mom and brothers. My mother enrolled in one of those resource center assistance programs and even began taking college courses. The resource center helped her find a moderate-paying job at a downtown bank. About five years ago, before my move to Delaware, Mom began attending church and is now a faithful member of the Victory City Fellowship Church. I think that's one of the main reasons why I attend with her so often. I want to help keep her on track. I'm also proud to say that she's been doing fantastic! No drugs and she has made me extremely proud of her.

Besides all of the past drama in my life, my job is very stressful. Being the only Black female in a growing computer company, I feel the constant scrutiny, however, I love my job. I wouldn't trade it for the world. I just know that I need to continue to take my certification courses if I want to stay on top of my game. Especially in such a male-dominated industry.

The waiter, or dare I say waitress, returned to our table.

"You ladies decide what you'd like to order?"

I ordered a White Zinfandel and Morgan ordered an apple martini.

I continued to flip through the menu and decided that I wanted an order of hot wings. Morgan and I split the order so I flagged for the waiter. He didn't see me, so I continued to wave and this rather fine gentleman, sitting in the back of the restaurant with two other guys waved at me as if I were greeting him. I gave him a quick nod and the waiter caught my eye and then the guy in the back realized I wasn't waving to him. He shrugged anyway and I smiled quickly and averted my attention to the waiter.

The waiter approached our table and I placed our order. Morgan decided she wanted something else to order. I looked up again and noticed the guy who had just waved looking at me very intently. Now most times I would look elsewhere, but for some reason I just continued to look at him with the same piercing gaze

"Be right back. Anything else I can get for you ladies?" the very good-looking, but very obviously gay waiter asked.

"No, thank you. Can you tell us what time the readings will begin?" I asked as I rejoined the conversation between Morgan and the waiter.

Only Fools Gamble Twice

"Sweetie, you know your cousins. CP time is when the show will start. Just relax and I'll bring your order and by the time you have your third drink, nothing will even matter," Mr. Thang said as he curled his lips and leaned on one leg.

"Okkkkayyy. How you *doin'*?" Morgan whispered to me, referring to the waiter's sexual preference.

"No. How you *doin'*?" Mr. Thang replied as he sauntered off to get us our drinks.

"I can't believe he heard me," Morgan said with her hand over her mouth.

"See, you need to stop talking about people," I replied as Morgan completely ignored me and began looking around the restaurant.

Mr. Thang returned in a few minutes with our order and true to his words by the time we had our third drink, I was feelin' it! I won't say that I was drunk, but I wasn't mad at anybody.

Finally, the emcee announced the first reader and everyone focused on the front of the stage. The first guy, a poet by the name of Dat' Baw Dave, was pretty good. He recited two poems, one titled, *Can I be that friend?* The second poem was about the whole R. Kelly situation. I was feeling his poems something terrible. I even purchased his CD when he came off the stage. Including Tina, there were seven readers. When Tina was up, she did one of her poems about friendship, tying our roots to the Motherland, of course. She also had some bongos playing as she performed a little African dance number to the beat. By the time she finished her poem, there was not a dry eye in the house, and everyone jumped up clapping, giving mad praise to the sista with the deep, passionate words. Once everyone calmed

down, and the final reader came out, we were all feeling the groove and the last woman ripped it up too.

"You know, I think I can get with this poetry thing here. The next time we come, I'm going to try to drop a little knowledge down on the mic," I said, leaning over to Morgan.

"Girl, hush. You know your ass ain't gettin' up on no damn stage, talking about nothing," Morgan responded.

"All right, you can sleep if you want to, but girl I got skills," I replied.

"Whatever."

"Please don't hate. Hate doesn't look good on you," I replied.

Although I was far from drunk, the effects of the drinks were making me feel extremely giddy and confident. When the emcee announced that it was now time for open mic, I instantly stood and walked up to the stage without looking back. Anyone who knows me understands that this isn't a strange occurrence for me. I'm known to jump up on stage in a hot New York minute. Now Morgan would soon eat her words. I was about to represent.

"What's your name, sugar?" the emcee asked.

"Taylor is what they call me," I said as I looked seductively over the crowd. I made eye contact with the guy in the rear of the restaurant. He sat forward in his chair and seemed to be looking through me. I returned the stare, as if I were the only person in the room. Our eyes locked and I don't think I ever stopped looking at him, not even to blink. It was like we were having a conversation without ever speaking a word.

Only Fools Gamble Twice

"What's the name of your poem, sugar?" the emcee asked.

"It's untitled. I'm going to freestyle about love," I said, still staring at Mr. Man in the back of the restaurant.

As I began my poem, I suddenly realized that I was standing in front of a crowd with nothing immediately coming to mind. What was I doing? I closed my eyes and tried to visualize exactly how I felt inside and how I wanted to express myself to the audience. I also had to regain my composure. I just didn't know how I got myself into these sorts of situations. I had to zone in and figure out how I would express myself to that special love, if I ever found him. For what seemed like an eternity I traveled through my mind, body, spirit, and soul and then I felt that I was ready. Or at least as ready as one could ever be in these types of situations.

To me, my love, you are my all in all.
With you by my side I feel ten feet tall.
In fact, I feel on top of the world
I pinch myself and ask, can this be real?
To me, my love, you are my yes when the world says no,
You are my sunshine in the rain,
My joy when there is pain.
Sweetheart, you are my Friday on a Monday, and I thank God for you each and every day.

When I finished my poem, the crowd stood, clapping and shouting. I returned the microphone to the emcee and exited the stage. Tina and Jared had joined Morgan and were seated at our table as I exited the stage.

"Damn, girl, I was supposed to be the professional, but I

see you have mad skills," Tina said playfully.

"I'm telling you. Taylor, where did you get that poem? I thought you were about to have a damn orgasm up there. Forget the damn apple martini, I better order me one of those drinks you're having. That was some powerful shit," Morgan said jokingly. Jared, who was normally quiet, also gave me my props.

The emcee made an announcement for the next person to come up and the guy I had made the serious eye contact with in the rear of the restaurant stepped up on the stage.

"What's your name, young brother?" the older gentleman asked. Mr. Man took the microphone and zeroed right in on me.

"They call me Delaney and the poem that I wish to relay to you all is also about love." The entire time he recited his poem, Delaney and I held a long and intense stare.

> *Upon the day that we meet, I must wait to feel what's in my heart.*
> *I feel like this will be meant to be,*
> *Me loving you and you loving me.*
> *When I feel your warm embrace I'll feel safe and secure.*
> *I'll feel sure of myself, who I am, why I'm here.*
> *Sweetness, my life with you I want to share.*
> *I want to share my mornings, afternoons, and evenings with you, doing what young lovers do*
> *Oh yes baby I do!*
> *To this woman, who I yearn to love,*
> *Close your eyes, look deep inside,*
> *Feel what I feel, know what I know,*
> *Then look into my eyes, enter my space*
> *Cause, baby, love is in your face!*

Again, the crowd went ballistic and Delaney was still eyeballing me until the emcee came onstage and took the microphone. Everyone was clapping and shouting, including me. To say that I was utterly impressed would have been the understatement of the millennium. I was also sexually aroused. I would never admit this to a soul, but his words, the way he moved his mouth, the tone of his voice, the way he looked at me, actually made the juices within flow through my body. It was surreal and I wanted to be that woman whom Delaney longed for in his poem.

"Is there something you want to tell me?" Morgan leaned over and asked as Delaney exited the stage.

When he walked past our table and while Morgan was questioning me, Delaney flashed a hell of a smile and winked at me. It wasn't that corny kind of wink, like those players give you, but one that asked, "Do you feel me?" And I was definitely feeling him.

"Hello. Earth to Taylor. Do you even hear me? This is some shit you see in the movies. What was that movie? *Love Jones?* This ain't no damn *Love Jones*," Morgan said as she pushed my arm.

"What do you mean? No, there's nothing to tell. I just see a guy and we make eye contact and that's that. No big deal," I said out loud, but knew that I really didn't mean that. It was definitely more than that.

I tried to act as if I were looking for the waiter, and just then I noticed Delaney and the two other guys he had been sitting with leave the club.

"Damn," I said, not realizing I had said it out loud.

"What's the matter with you?" Morgan asked as she followed my eyes. "Damn is right. He is fine as a motherfucker too. Oh sorry, I forgot, my mouth," Morgan said, as she placed her hand over her mouth.

"Girlfriend, I ain't one to do a whole bunch of cussing, but he was fine as a motherfucker!" I said as Morgan and I shared an old-fashioned high-five.

Tina and Jared were talking with some friends, and Morgan and I had decided we were still feeling the vibe and wanted to check out Bluezette on Market Street. We figured we'd hit the Butter Cup Lounge some other time. I just wasn't ready to drive thirty minutes while my groove was still going. Bluezette has the best R&B and jazz in town and catered to a mature clientele. We invited Gina and Jared, but we knew they would decline so we made our way to the parking area. Plus, I knew they were due for a few puffs on that weed. I really had to talk to that sista when I got a chance. She has to stop that crap. She smokes way too much.

As we left Warm Daddy's, we noticed Byron was working overtime so we grabbed Morgan's keys and tried to maneuver our way out of the crowded parking lot. I tried to take my mind off the guy who had stimulated my interest, but Morgan wasn't having it.

"Maybe next Friday he'll be here again. I'm supposed to go out of town next week I should be back early on Friday, but I'll let you know," Morgan said as we headed the five blocks in her car to Bluezette.

What's done is done. If it were meant to be it would have been. If I see him again then that's another story, but I'm not

Only Fools Gamble Twice

going to break my neck to try to see him again. If he wanted to get to know me he would have come over to our table," I said, trying to believe my own words. There was something about this guy that really had me going.

He was probably somebody's baby's father, some woman's husband or worse, some man's man. A guy who looked that good had to be tied and chained down to somebody.

When we arrived at Bluezette, Morgan and I felt right at home. Since I was extremely tired from working all week, I promised myself that I would have just two drinks and I was determined to be out. Morgan is a dancing fool at heart and the smooth jazz was right up her alley. Most of the time she didn't even need a dance partner, she would just start doing this Caribbean type of dance and the whole crowd would cheer her on. As if she needed more attention to add to her dynamic personality. On second thought, make that crazy personality.

We were lucky to find a table near the VIP section. Morgan was dancing and walking to our table, and it wasn't long before some baldhead guy had her on the dance floor, shaking everything in her family tree. I waved for the waitress and she gave me a sign that told me she was busy and to hold on.

As I waited patiently for the waitress, I noticed a presence at my side.

"Do you mind if I sit here and talk with you?" I looked up to a very handsome Delaney. The man. My man...I mean the guy who had shared that intense look with me and the one who made my knees shake.

He looked even better up close and personal. He appeared to be in his late twenties, definitely YTM (Young Tender Morsel) material. He had the prettiest set of teeth this

side of Dionne Warwick; almond- shaped; jet-black eyes; and jet-black, wavy hair. He was about six feet four inches, very pleasing to the eye, and had a muscular build. I had to remind myself to keep my composure. I also had to remember, he was probably involved with someone.

"Sure, have a sit down," I said as I flashed my million-dollar smile. I didn't wear braces for three years for nothing. What's a little hospitality? I reminded myself not to be too friendly until I found out his 411.

"I'd like to formally introduce myself. As you may remember, my name is Delaney Love, and you are Taylor, but I didn't get a last name," Delaney said, peering into my eyes.

This time it was very different. His eyes were dancing and smiling. I felt so connected to this guy, like I had known him for years. *Stay focused, girl!*

"Chavers. Taylor Chavers," I said as I extended my hand.

For the second time that night, my hand was kissed, but it was definitely not the same type of kiss that I got from Byron earlier that night. Although it was just on the hand, Delaney's lips were soft as Georgia peaches and at that moment I wished that I could trade my lips for my hand.

"What are you drinking?" Delaney asked.

"I was trying to get the waitress a few minutes ago, but I see she's still running around."

"I'll go to the bar. What are you drinking?" he asked again.

"Chardonnay," I responded.

"Pretty and good taste too," Delaney said as he flashed his killer smile at me. "Be right back." As he walked away, I was able

Only Fools Gamble Twice

to really check the brother out.
	From the back, he had what appeared to be a rock-hard ass, broad shoulders, and a confident walk--not conceited, but a guy who had a lot going on for himself. When he returned, he had two glasses of Chardonnay. As he set the glasses down, I happened to notice that his left hand, third ring finger was without a wedding band, but we all know that doesn't mean a damn thing!
	So, tell me, how did you become involved with poetry?" Delaney asked.
	"Actually, my girlfriend invited us down tonight. She was the one before the end who ripped it up. I don't write poetry. I'm a writer at heart and I haven't written anything substantial since my college years," I responded.
	"What college did you attend?" Delaney asked.
	"I graduated from Lincoln University with a degree in computer science," I said and took a sip of my drink.
	"Oh yeah, a few of my frat brothers graduated from Lincoln. A guy name Wendell Prailow, brother by the name of Keith Scott, and Horace Bryant," Delaney stated.
	"I know Horace. He was in a few of my classes. Really nice guy. He actually married one of my sorors. A girl name Kelly," I responded.
	"Yeah-yeah, I went to their wedding," Delaney said.
	"Really?" I said, sounding surprised. "I was there too. They had about four hundred guests, so there's no telling who was there. Really nice, but really too big for my taste," I said.
	"So you're a member of what fraternity?" I asked.
	"Omega Psi Phi Fraternity, Inc.," Delaney said. "And you're a member of what sorority?"
	"Zeta Phi Beta," I responded as I took a sip of my drink.

"Small world. My mother's one of your sorors. My mother will definitely love you now," he said as he looked at me with those piercing brown eyes.

"Oh, really? I mean that's nice that your mom's a fellow soror and I love her for that, but what makes you think I'm going to meet her?" I asked as I leaned forward on one elbow.

"Because I'd like you to meet her--after we have dinner a few times, of course," Delaney said as he leaned on one elbow, his face now about four inches in front of mine.

"Now tell me who told you I would go out to dinner with you? You're mighty confident, I see," I said, not breaking my position.

"You're right. I am confident that you'll go out to dinner with me. We just have to work out all the details later on. But for now, let's just say we'll talk and get to know each other. We'll discuss the dinner at a later time," Delaney said as he looked down and took my hand in his.

I couldn't help but feel powerless in his presence. I especially felt that his hand was that of a true man, and although he simply held mine in his, I felt that he could protect me against anything at that very moment.

"So you're not married?" I cautiously questioned. Here I was sitting here already holding hands with this man. I held my breath as I waited for the answer.

"Never been fortunate enough. I recently got back from California. I've been traveling since I graduated from grad school and I haven't had the time to devote to a serious relationship," Delaney responded.

"Oh, okay, so you're a playa-playa?" I asked, becoming a

Only Fools Gamble Twice

little annoyed.

"No, not at all. Like I said, with me traveling and working long hours to set up my company's computer mainframe, I just haven't had the time for a long-lasting relationship. We have offices in thirty-eight cities and I've been traveling all over the country setting up these new systems. To be honest, I've only had two meaningful relationships. Last year I was involved in a serious relationship with a woman I'd met in college. We tried to make the long-distance thing work out, but that didn't last too long. She eventually got tired of traveling all over the country to visit me or vice versa, so eventually she broke it off and went back home to Hampton. I can't say that I blame her. I wanted a future with her, but I want to be able to establish my career so I can offer my wife and children something more one day.

She didn't want to wait and I didn't want to settle for anything less. I don't want to struggle like a dog like my father and mother had to in order to put a decent meal in my family's stomach and a roof over our heads. I love my parents. They were married for more than twenty-five years, but they worked like crazy to put my two sisters and me through school and to raise us to strive just that much harder," Delaney said, hunching his shoulders.

"Besides, we were too young anyway. I think my ex prepared me to be the man that my future wife will be proud of one day. I got nothing but love for her," Delaney said as he looked forward and took another sip of his drink.

For some odd reason I believed him. Not that it's so odd. There's this terrible myth that all men are dogs. I do believe that there are still plenty of good men out there. I have to if I want to be married with children one day. I simply cannot feed into the

hype that my husband will be an asshole--at least not all of the time.

"So what's your story? I don't see a ring on your finger, but as good as you look, I can't imagine that you don't have some strong boyfriend waiting at home for you," Delaney said.

"Well that tells you something about looks then. Because I'm not seeing anyone seriously right now," I responded.

"Well if I have anything to say about that, you won't be able to say that too much longer," he said, a little too confidently, yet again.

"Excuse me? What makes you think that you have any say in that matter? Who says that I'm looking for a serious relationship?" I questioned with my hand on my hip.

I wasn't mad or even slightly annoyed, I just didn't want brother man to think I was some desperate sista out to scoop up some man in a club or something.

"Well for the record, you said you're looking for a serious relationship," he responded as he gulped the last of his wine as he flagged the waitress. "Would you care for another drink?"

"Yes, but I'll get this round," I responded and fished through my purse to get my wallet.

"Please, that won't be necessary. I thank you for the offer, but I'll get it," Delaney said as he placed his hand over mine. Seriously, I've got this, but thanks for the offer. You don't meet too many women out here who would even suggest that they would buy a man a drink," Delaney said as he looked at me intently.

Having him buy my drinks was a big problem with me because I don't like for guys to keep paying my way. I don't want them to think I owe them anything. My grandmother once told me to never take any money from a guy. I know this sounds crazy in this day, but I'd rather be independent any day of the week. The house that I own I got that, the car I'm driving...you get the picture. When it's time for a man to roll, let him do so, but he'll never be able to say he bought me a damn thing. However, I figured a few drinks were not a big deal.

"So tell me, when did I say I was looking for a relationship?" I asked to change the subject.

"In your poem. Don't you remember? You want the same thing most people want: love. It's just a matter of finding that perfect match," Delaney said as the waitress reached our table and he ordered another round.

We continued to talk about school and our careers. Delaney graduated from Hampton University and received his master's from the Penn State University. We had actually grown up in the same South Philadelphia neighborhood, but had never seen each other.

We also realized that although we both liked sports--he was a basketball fan and I was a football fan. I explained to Delaney how much I loved sports, however, basketball was just one that I couldn't get into. I had to admit that I hated the game, but loved to look at the men. I used to have this guy who lived in the same complex with me who played for the Sixers. He thought he was all that and just swore that all of the girls were falling all over him. His attitude made me ignore him just that much more. If it's one thing I hate it's a guy who thinks he's prettier than me. So every time I saw him, I just completely ignored him. I think he probably wasn't used to women ignoring him, so that made him try that much harder. I almost started to go out with him, but I found out he had a pregnant girlfriend and was hitting on this other girl who lived in our complex. Needless to say, that was it for me.

"So tell me, you were really into that poem tonight. Where does that passion originate?" I asked as I leaned forward. Delaney's great smelling cologne was driving me crazy.

"It comes from being alone so much. It comes from wanting something so bad and not being able to find what you're looking for. It's built-up energy that I have that I want to release, but it's just so difficult finding someone on the same page as you. While I was traveling, I won't lie to you, I met a lot of women, but when I tried to challenge them intellectually, they had nothing of which to speak. I would try to talk about politics, world hunger, anything, and they couldn't stimulate my mind. A lot of men will think that's not a problem, but you want to be able to hold a decent conversation with someone from time to time. That's why if you notice, when you got on stage to do your thing, I was checking you out and was thinking, *Who is this woman, and where is her energy coming from?* I was also thinking I could feel and identify with your thoughts before you uttered one word. That's why I may seem confident that we're going to connect in some way, maybe not anything serious--that's to be determined-- but at least if nothing more, I've found someone who can at least hold a conversation with me. When you recited your poem I felt what was moving inside of you," Delaney explained.

"Damn," was all that I could say.

It was as if everything that I felt onstage was seen by him and only him. As if I had been that transparent, that he could tell what I was thinking. I didn't know if that was a good thing or not, but it was nice to meet someone who understood my inner person.

"So, Ms. Taylor, since we've talked about just about everything under the sun, would you say that you're ready to dance with me?" Delaney asked.

"I only save dances for the guys who can actually dance. Would that be you?" I teased as I stood, not waiting for a response. I grabbed him by the hand and led him to the dance floor. While we danced, I noticed that not only was the brother smart, good-looking, and utterly sexy, he could actually dance and we were kicking it. Just then the deejay announced that he was slowing things down. Delaney grabbed me by my waist as we began slow dancing to "Let's Get Married."

"Let's," Delaney whispered in my ear.

"Let's what?" I whispered in return, slightly confused.

"Nothing," Delaney pulled me tighter and we continued to share the warmness and the frustration we obviously both had been feeling. It had been a long time since I had been held so closely by a man who a) looked good, b) smelled good, and c) felt so damn good.

"Ms. Taylor, I don't know who you are or how you did it so fast, but I like you. A lot," Delaney whispered closely in my ear.

That was enough to send me into cardiac arrest. Little did he know that my ear was one of my weak spots. At that moment, I knew what people meant by love at first sight.

Whew was all that I could say as I leaned on Delaney's firmly toned shoulder and allowed myself to really feel our souls connect.

2/MORGAN

I was on the dance floor with this very good-looking guy named Derrick, and we were vibin'. D.J. Ran was playing all of my favorite songs and from the looks of things, Derrick was enjoying himself too. We must have danced for about an hour straight before the music slowed down. Since I make it a rule never to slow dance with men I don't personally know in a club or men with foul breath. Man Derrick was cute, but when he asked my name, I had to step back. I offered the brother a breath mint, but he declined. I wanted to say: "No, please! I insist. You can't possibly decline my offer," but I didn't. I just popped one in my mouth and turned my head. After a few more minutes, Derrick kept trying to hold a conversation and I wasn't having it.

The next thing I know, this bastard picks up his cell phone and pressed his hand over his other ear and starts talking on the damn phone while we're dancing. Between the liquor and my outspoken attitude, I was afraid that I was bound to say something. I didn't want to start any drama, so I finally walked away and left his stupid ass on the dance floor with his tired-ass cell phone, breath, and conversation.

I thought the man looked good, but I don't usually go after extremely fine men because they come with too much baggage. I believe that if you think your man looks extremely good, then he, along with the rest of the single female population, thinks the same way and those are problems that I can live without. Besides, the brother's breath smelled as if a dog died on his tongue. It was foul and nasty, just foul and nasty.

I made my way through the crowd and was checking out

all of the diverse brothers in the club. *Damn, this place is jam packed tonight* I thought. The men were definitely in here. It ain't nothing like seeing a bunch of positive brothers coming together. The sight of all of the diversity left me almost speechless.

I noticed Taylor on the dance floor, all wrapped up in some guy's arms. Strange, even for Taylor. *Maybe she knows him.* I thought. I was still breaking my neck to see who he was, when I noticed it was the guy from Warm Daddy's. "What?" I said out loud. What luck. I didn't think we'd ever see him again. *Girlfriend better watch it,* I thought. Just like an old boyfriend used sing a particular portion of Lisa Fischer's song, *How can I ease the pain*—he used to sing the part that goes *a fool for love is a fool for pain,* all the time. It wasn't until we broke up that I realized he was trying to tell me something—the bastard.

I used the ladies' room, washed my hands, fixed my hair and applied more lipstick. As I stepped outside the bathroom, I collided with a dark-brown man who appeared to be in his early thirties.

"Oh, my goodness, I am so very sorry. I should have been watching where I was going," the man said in what appeared to be an African accent.

"No, no, it's really no problem. I should have been paying attention," I said.

"I really apologize. Please let me buy you a drink," the man said. He was not all that in the looks department, but definitely not ugly, just average looking. He was about six-one, wore glasses, and when he smiled he had a huge gap between his two front teeth.

"Sure, why not? I guess that's the least you can do since

you almost knocked me down," I said jokingly.

"Oh, a woman with a sense of humor? By the way, my name is Kofie," he said, extending his hand.

"Pleased to meet you, Kofie. My name is Morgan," I said as Kofie led me past the bar and up the stairs to a table in the VIP section. Hmm, well at least he was not the average Joe. The brother had style and class. I tried to remember where I had seen him before.

"You look familiar. Were you at Warm Daddy's earlier tonight?" I asked. Before he answered, it occurred to me I had noticed him earlier at Warm Daddy's with the very same guy who was now dancing with Taylor.

"Yes, I was there with a few guys. Your friend and my associate really hit it off rather well. We haven't seen him since you two walked in this place," Kofie said, pointing toward the dance floor at the obvious lovebirds.

"You mentioned your associate. You two are not friends?" I asked.

"We're friends through a mutual friend, William. He's around here somewhere. Oh, here he is right now," Kofie said, as a shorter gentleman approached our table.

"Hey, Kof, man, I'm out. I have to get up early in the morning. I have some business to handle. I'll see or talk to you later on this weekend. Excuse me," William said as Kofie stood and shook his hand.

"William, this is Morgan. Morgan, this is a my very good friend, William," Kofie said.

"Good to meet you. Listen, man, tell Dee I'll holla at him later on in the weekend. You two have a good time. Now if you'll

Only Fools Gamble Twice

excuse me, I'm headed home to get some much-needed rest," William said as he gave us a quick wave and was on his way.

When the waitress came by Kofie ordered a bottle of Belvedere. *This brother is definitely blazin'*, I thought.

"So tell me, did you enjoy the poetry reading tonight?" Kofie asked.

"I had a really enjoyable time. It was my first time attending one of those readings, but it definitely won't be my last. Besides, my girl Taylor truly represented tonight," I remarked.

"I see. Do you ever write poetry?"

"No, I'll leave that to Taylor. That's definitely not my forte. What does your name mean?" I asked, changing the subject.

"In the language of Swahili, it means a handful," Kofie said proudly.

"And are you?" I asked seriously.

"Well that is to hopefully be judged by you. I can only hope that I am not too easy to figure out because that would take all of the fun out of getting to know me. For the record, I'd like to think I have a sense of humor, but I take many things seriously. I have an agenda. There are certain things I want out of life. I know that if I work hard now, then I can sit back and relax later on. Right now I have about six more years left to my game plan. I wish to retire at the age of forty," Kofie explained.

"Sounds very interesting, but I don't know that I would want to retire at such a young age," I replied.

"See, that's the problem with you Americans. You all do not share the same work ethic of many people from other countries. Why would you want to work until your sixties? By that time, I plan to be traveling around the world. Right now I work three jobs and I have several investments. At the age of forty, my hard work will allow me to live the life that I want," Kofie continued.

"How do you know what my work ethic is? You've known me for what, five minutes? To be honest with you, everyone who I know is a hardworking, college graduate and wants something more for themselves out of life. Both my parents are college educated, and the family members that I have who did not go to college work just as hard as anyone I know. For me, I just can't see myself traveling and relaxing for the next thirty or forty years. I actually enjoy what I do. I enjoy going to work and interacting with the people there. Don't get me wrong, it can get very stressful sometimes, but I have the type of personality that I would become extremely bored if I had to stay at home," I explained.

"Let me ask you this question: are you married?" he asked.

"No, I don't think I'm quite ready to be married," I answered.

"Oh, my goodness! Why would you say such a thing? In my county, we are married early and begin building our lives for our future. I asked if you were married because you said you wouldn't want to stay at home. What if your husband wanted you to stay at home and raise your children while he earned the income?" Kofie asked.

"Never!" I exclaimed.

"My word! Again, why not? Why would you want some stranger to raise your kids while you went off to work?" Kofie asked, seeming to become somewhat annoyed.

"It's not about having a stranger raising my kids. First, I have parents who could help me out with watching my children. Secondly, my parents have been married for more than thirty years. Both my mother and father have careers and were able to raise two educated and independent young ladies. There's no way that I'm going to be financially dependent on my husband. Now if my child were ill and needed me to be there, then of course I would do what I have to do, but as long as I'm able to work, then that's what I'm going to do," I responded confidently.

"See again, there's another problem with American women. You all don't trust your men. I think you American women don't trust men enough to become financially dependent as you say. In my country, a man marries a woman and they are married forever. There's no such thing as divorce and the man running off to leave his family without a means of support," Kofie explained.

"You may have a point there. Fifty years ago, pretty much the same rule applied here. People got married and stayed married. My grandparents were married for more than sixty-five years; through thick and thin. If a couple argued constantly, they worked it out. If they weren't happy in their marriage, they worked it out. Today, more than fifty percent of marriages end in divorce. People don't want to work out their problems," I responded.

"See, that proves my point. I think because women are no longer financially dependent on their husbands, like they were fifty years ago, then they have other means to remove themselves from the marriage. If your grandfather made your grandmother unhappy she had no choice but to stay in the marriage. Where would she go with all of her children and no money to support herself? There was no one who would even support her in that decision. These days it's so easy to get divorced. That's why I think in my country, it helps that the wife stays at home, while the husband goes out and earns the income," Kofie explained.

"Yeah, but let me ask you, how many of those husbands are being faithful? See, don't get me wrong, I love my grandparents and my parents and they both have many years in their respective marriages, but I know for a fact that my mother and grandmother endured many sleepless nights, due to their husband's infidelity. What could they do? Where were they going? How unhappy do you think they were, knowing their husbands were off fooling around with some other woman when they could do nothing about it?" I asked, now becoming annoyed with this topic.

"I see what you're saying, but in my country, that's the way it works. I'm not saying that I agree, but it's just something that is not spoken about, at all. You marry and you stay married, until death parts you, period. End of story, everyone is happy, nobody gets hurt. How about we talk about something else because I can see we could be on this topic forever. You make for a very good conversation. I'd like to get to know you a bit more. Trust me, not to sound overly sure of myself, but I'm worth getting to know. I promise you that much," Kofie responded.

"Tell me what makes you so special?" I inquired.

"Now is not the time or place, but I assure you that I am like no other you've ever met before," Kofie stated.

I simply said nothing. It wasn't that I was speechless, because that would have been a first for me. I've heard men proclaim all of the great things they can do one time too many, but when it was time to step up to the plate, well as the saying goes, they could talk the talk but couldn't walk the walk. With Kofie, he was pretty sure of himself, but not in a conceited sort of way. I had to watch this one. He wasn't your average type of guy.

We continued to sip on the champagne and talked for what seemed like hours as we got to know each other. Kofie explained how he had been in the states for twelve years and how he had struggled to get his bachelor's degree from Columbia University, then his master's from Penn State University, while supporting himself and his family members who were back in Cameroon, Africa. He told me how he was currently working two full-time jobs and helping out his cousin at their African clothing business in New York.

"Wow. Do you ever stop to breathe or sleep? You seem to keep going and going. You remind me a little of myself. My parents are always remarking how I'm always on the run and into something," I stated.

"Tell me about yourself, Morgan. You have such a pretty name, and you are definitely a very beautiful woman. I've been babbling on and on for about ten minutes now. I want to know everything there is to know about you," Kofie said enthusiastically.

"Well let's see, as I stated earlier, I'm a SINC woman," I began.

"Oh, I know, single-income no children, am I right?" Kofie said proudly.

"Exactly. I'm an account manager for Beckerman and Leechum, a large pharmaceutical company in downtown Wilmington. As you can see, I'm pretty outspoken and independent, and I have a no-nonsense attitude about life," I explained.

"Tell me why are you so tough? I think behind that tough exterior is a warm and friendly woman just screaming to come out," Kofie said with a huge grin.

"I don't know about all of the screaming to come out stuff. You can break my heart, but never my spirit." I responded.

"Oh, well, I see you need some TLC," Kofie said.

"Ah, let me see. You're just the guy to heal my wounded heart," I said, clutching my chest.

"Only if that is your wish. I can just tell you have this tough woman role down to a science and it's pretty obvious you're a very sweet person. Hopefully, you'll soon see that I'm not about a whole bunch of games. I don't have time for that with my schedule and the life that I want," Kofie explained.

"I guess I need to get used to saying it, but I broke up with my boyfriend of three years recently," I explained to Kofie.

"Oh, this sounds interesting. Why would any man be so foolish to be apart from you?" Kofie asked.

Since Mister and I broke up six months ago, everyone has wanted to know what happened. I even have to ask myself that question sometimes. Mister and I had been seeing each other for three years. I had just received my job at Beckerman and Leechum. I met Mister one day while having lunch with a coworker at The Christiana River Club, a black-owned club and restaurant downtown. I had seen Mister several times with a guy named Omar, a former classmate of mine at Delaware State University. One day I noticed Omar sitting by himself at Rodney Square Mall and I asked him where his friend had been for the last

-42-

Only Fools Gamble Twice

couple of days.

Omar said that it was funny that I had asked about Mister because he had been asking Omar to hook a brother up for several months. Since I love a good-looking man as well as the next woman, I told Omar to introduce us the next time he saw me on the Square. The following week, Omar introduced us and a year later Mister and I were a serious item, or at least I thought so.

After two years of serious dating, Mister and I decided to rent a two-bedroom town house together and had spoken of marriage and even began looking at engagement rings.

I really thought Mister and I would be together forever. I know that it sounds corny, but I honestly thought I had found my soul mate. We would stay up for hours on end, knowing we each had to get up early for work, but that never stopped our long talks about the future. Since neither of us have children, we spent every waking moment outside of work together, taking weekend trips to various intriguing places. We traveled to Madrid, Belize, and even took a trip to Paris. I'm not lying when I tell you that I loved this man more than he loved himself. He was truly my best friend.

Suddenly, he changed out of the clear blue. One morning, I was running late for work. Mister was downstairs sitting at the kitchen table reading the paper. I knew that I was late, but I wanted to throw some bacon in the pan and a few waffles in the toaster for my baby. I never liked sending him out of the door on an empty stomach.

I can still see his nonchalant face as if the incident happened yesterday. I should have known that it was going to be a bad day when his bad-ass cat ran up and put a rip in my stockings. I could have killed that little pussy...cat. Anyway, as I turned to run back upstairs and tried unsuccessfully to kick the cat square in his ass, Mister looked up from his newspaper and said, way too calmly for my taste, "I've been thinking,"

"Hold on, sweetie I'll be right back. Howie just tore my stockings I'll be right back in a minute."

"That can wait. Come have a seat right here."

I thought of protesting, but the look on his face told me this was serious.

"What's up, baby?" I asked as I attempted to sit on his lap.

"No. Sit over there in that chair."

"What's your problem?" I asked, now becoming irritated. It's one thing that I hate and that's to be pushed away like I'm some annoying pest.

"I just want to talk with you. The lease is up at the end of the month, right?" he asked.

"Yeah, we talked about going in to sign a new lease. You know that."

"Well I've been thinking lately. I need some time and space to think things through. We need to call the realtor and let them know we won't be renewing the lease. I'm moving out at the end of the month."

Just like that! No explanation, no thoughts about how my day would turn out, just said what he said and that was that. I cried and pleaded for him to explain what I had done. I was ready to change or take back anything that I had said. I ended up calling in sick something that I rarely do. I climbed back in bed, crying and feeling devastated all day. Mister went on to work as if nothing was up. That night when he came home he still said nothing. That same evening, he even moved all of his belongings into the other bedroom. For two weeks our conversations were very limited. I was the one trying to discuss the situation with him, but he wouldn't even tell me what was wrong. I was frustrated and my nerves were a wreck. My whole hairline fell out around my edges and I lost ten pounds in a few days. After a week of the silent treatment, I began to become angry and irritated. I went from hurt to a woman scorned, and we all know the result of that.

    I will admit, I've had a pretty good upbringing with lots of attention from my family, but I must have been dropped on my head when I was younger, because I can turn into a crazed woman when I'm pushed. I'm also pretty understanding and genuinely a nice person, but don't push me.

    One night, as I lay in bed crying, Mister came into my room and held me closely. He wiped my tears away and we made the most passionate love known to man. I felt wonderful. All of the feelings that I had for him came out of me that evening. I fell asleep in his arms and it was the most peaceful sleep that I had since the beginning of the whole ordeal. I believed he just needed time to himself. Whatever had been on his mind was now over and he had come to his senses.

    When I awakened early that next morning, my eyes were swollen from all of the crying I had done and Mister was not in bed. I went downstairs to find him. He was sitting at the kitchen table eating breakfast and reading a newspaper.

    "Hey, baby, why didn't you wake me? Where's my breakfast?" I asked, trying to wake up and get myself together as I looked in the stove for my meal.

"Hey," Mister responded coldly, not looking up from the newspaper. I looked at him strangely. I just couldn't understand why he was in such a foul mood.

"I didn't have time to make you breakfast. Oh yeah, my car is down, and I need a ride today. I have an appointment to see about an apartment. You think you can take me to go see it this morning?" Mister asked nonchalantly.

"WHAT THE FUCK DID YOU JUST SAY? YOU'RE GOING TO LOOK FOR A FUCKING APARTMENT? WHAT THE HELL WAS LAST NIGHT ABOUT?" I screamed at the top of my lungs, pissed as all hell.

"Look, just calm the hell down. Stop cussing at me. Last night doesn't change a damn thing. Did I promise you anything? Did I?" Mister responded, raising his voice as well.

"I don't believe this shit. Why are you doing this?" I demanded.

"Just forget it. You know what, forget I even asked you for a ride. I'll be out of here before the end of the week," he said as he stood, slammed the paper down on the table, and walked past me.

I didn't know what to do. Before I knew it, I pushed him so hard, he fell into the wall. He didn't even miss a beat. He just turned around and gave me the coldest stare. He chuckled and then went upstairs. At first I thought of following him, but my legs wouldn't allow it. I simply fell to my knees and began to relive all those terrible feelings. If you've ever been in love with someone, you know that it's so easy to fall in love, but so hard to recover from the devastation love can sometimes leave behind. It was too early to call my sister, so I called the only other person I could who would listen to my problems. I called my mom.

My mom picked up on the second ring, as she always did.

"God loves you," my mother said smoothly into the phone.

"Mom, it's me," I said. Hearing her voice made me just want to burst out in tears.

"What's wrong?" she asked.

"He's trippin', Mom. I don't know what the heck is going on with him. He just told me he would be out by the end of the week. How does he think he can just walk away from our relationship after three years without so much as an explanation? I can't take it anymore. I'm about to flip out," I said as the tears began to roll down my face.

"Hang in there, baby. You're going to be just fine. There has to be a reason why he's acting this way. When he's ready, he'll talk to you. You know he loves you and I would bet he's not planning to go anywhere. I would be very surprised if he did. But if he does, you make sure you can cover your expenses and live the way you've been living while he's been there," Mom cautioned.

"Oh, I'm no fool. I have a pretty huge savings. I'll be fine financially. It's just that I don't get this. We were talking about marriage and now this?" I said, confused as ever.

"Honey, sometimes we question these things, but it could be a blessing in disguise. Maybe he's not the man for you. I know it's hard and it doesn't make you feel any better to say this, but this, too, shall pass. I promise you, you will not feel this way forever. It gets easier to deal with. Trust me on that. I love your father dearly, but we've had our downs, too, and don't think I don't know how you feel. I just wish there was something I could do to take away the pain," Mom said, her voice providing some comfort.

Mom and I continued to talk until, for the moment, my tears dried and she even had me laughing by the end of our conversation.

True to his word, Mister moved out at the end of the week. For about four months, he continued to string me along, and I allowed it. Behaving like a true damn fool in love. He'd call every night and we'd sometimes have the best conversations. As soon as I questioned him about us, he'd get all upset, telling me that I was ruining what we were building all over again. I would often go to his house for dinner and he would come over to mine. Nothing more than just good company and great food.

One night, after we hung up from talking on the phone, he told me he was going to bed, I decided to surprise him at his door with a black negligee, thigh-high stockings, and black high-heeled shoes. I put on my trench coat and sashayed myself on over to Mister's place. Let's face it, a sista has needs too. I figured it was time I took charge of this relationship. Show him, so to speak, what I was working with. He was extremely happy to see me and the romance was great, just like I had remembered it, but the following day, I got the cold treatment.

It seemed that sex meant nothing to him. He could just turn himself on and then return to the mean person I had come to know. I couldn't blame him. It was my fault and I was equally to blame. You see I was playing a game of pussy power. You know women do it all of the time. We often use what's between our legs to get a man to respond to our needs and for me it just wasn't working. Now the way that I see it is that I had several choices. I could either stop playing the game altogether; play the game and not get played, which should be left to professionals who know what they're doing; or take the good with the bad. I know that sex doesn't mean the same thing for men as it does for women. One just can't get caught up. So, I decided to get out of the game completely and move on.

Another night Mister called me and asked me to come over and I said that I would, but I never went. Instead, I went out and purchased a friend of my own from one of those erotica stores... if you catch my drift, so my sexual frustrations were partially relieved. After that, I had to completely cut him off. I got Caller ID, so I would know not to answer his call. I could no longer allow him to have his cake and eat it, too, literally speaking. The longer I revealed my vulnerability, the longer he would use that to his advantage. Don't get me wrong, it was the hardest thing I've had to do, but it was for my own good.

Even now, Mister calls me and still tries to either stop by or have me come over to his apartment, but I am slowly getting over him. He still won't explain what went wrong with our relationship and I refuse to be used by anyone. Enough is enough.

I must have been daydreaming because Kofie was still waiting for an answer.

"Hello. Earth to Morgan. I was asking you why a man would be so foolish as to be apart from you?" Kofie asked again.

"It's a long story, and I'll be sure to tell you one day, if there is a one day. But to leave things as is, I am very much single," I replied.

"Glad to hear that, and if I have anything to do with that, there will definitely be a one day," Kofie said, displaying a sincere smile, something I had not seen in a while.

"I hope so too," I said. For the first time in nine months I started feeling alive again.

3/TAYLOR

    I was really looking for Morgan now. Delaney wanted to go to a twenty-four-hour restaurant to get something to eat so we could talk and not shout to be heard. I don't usually meet a man in a club and just go off with him, but for some reason, like I said, I felt a connection with Delaney and I wanted to know more about him.

    I haven't been seriously involved with a lot of men. I'm always too busy having fun or I just find a way to keep busy, which never leaves me with a whole lot of time to get my feelings entangled in any one man. Don't get me wrong, I love men and I love to be with them. I just never found that true love to make you do crazy things where you fall completely head over heels. Something tells me my experience with Delaney will be different, like he could be that guy who I would bend over backwards to please. You know the kind of guy you do cartwheels and back flips to make happy. I know several women who all their man has to do is just think they wanted something and their woman had it for them before the man finished the thought. Delaney looked like the kind of guy I could trust with my heart, soul, and much more. When I looked at him standing there, helping me look for Morgan, the chemistry between us just felt so right.

    Delaney and I found Morgan talking to some guy in the VIP section of the club. I figured, knowing Morgan, the girl who knew everyone, she had probably run into someone she knew. Despite being impatient at times, Morgan could just meet someone and instantly hit it off with that person, acting as if she had known him for years. Whenever we go out, I'm usually on my

Only Fools Gamble Twice

own. I swear that girl either knows everyone in the world, or she's going to die trying to meet the people she doesn't already know. She's just a social butterfly.

"Hey, girl. What's up? Listen up. Delaney, this is my girl Morgan," I said.

"Pleased to meet you, Morgan," Delaney said, giving a nod.

"I see you two have met," Delaney said, looking at Morgan and the guy she was sitting with at the table.

"Oh, you two know each other?" I asked Delaney, looking confused.

"Yeah, this is Kofie. We were at Warm Daddy's together earlier."

Just then, it dawned on me that Delaney was with two other guys and Kofie was one of them. Funny how you can see someone and not see them. All of my attention was focused on Delaney. Who could blame me?

"Kofie, this is Taylor," Morgan said.

"Nice meeting you," we both said at the same time.

"Taylor and I have decided to get something to eat. Would you two like to join us?" Delaney Morgan and Kofie.

"As a matter of fact that sounds like a great idea. We'd like to join you two," Kofie responded.

"*Excuse me.* How do you know that I would like to get something to eat?" Morgan asked with a hand on her hip.

"Oh, I apologize. Would you like to join your friend and my man here and get something to eat?" Kofie asked, looking embarrassed.

"Sure, why not? I'm starving," Morgan responded as she

quickly stood and gulped down the remainder of her drink. We all began laughing.

Morgan must always get the last word. At first I would try to challenge her, but it made no sense. My girl is downright ornery.

"Well then, I guess we're off to get some chow. Hold up. Where's Bill?" Delaney asked Kofie.

"Oh, he said he would talk to you later on this weekend. He actually left a while ago. He had to get up early and handle some business," Kofie replied

Delaney reached for my hand and we headed for the door. We told Morgan and Kofie that we would meet them by the entrance because Delaney wanted to run to the men's room before we left.

After Delaney exited the bathroom he ran into a guy he knew and they spoke briefly. As he was approaching me a woman who appeared to have had one too many drinks staggered by and then abruptly stopped in the middle of the floor, turned around, and staggered over to where we were standing.

"Ah-ah, I know you ain't leaving, baby. Who gon' buy me a drink? The party is just gettin' started," the drunken woman hollered in a slurred voice.

"Ah, sweetheart, I think you had one too many drinks already. Do you have a ride home?" Delaney asked the woman in a concerned voice.

"Why you all up in my business? That shit don't concern you no way. For your information, I'm here with my baby fatha and yeah he got a car, so stay the fuck out of my business. I mean damn, a sista ask a brotha to buy her a damn drink and he think she want him to be her next baby daddy," the woman rambled on in a drunken slur.

Then as suddenly as she had appeared, the woman staggered off to return to a man at a nearby table who I assumed was her baby's father.

"Taylor, you see what brothers got to go through? I mean was I wrong? I don't mind if a woman drinks, but there comes a time where you have to draw a line," Delaney said, appearing to be upset by what had transpired.

"Don't worry about it, sweetie. It's fine," I replied as I grabbed his hand.

"Hold on. Say that again. I like the way you call me sweetie. I think I could get used to that," Delaney responded, obviously forgetting about the drunken woman.

I began to blush. "Oh, you like, sweetie? Then I've got tons more for you. Come on let's bounce. Morgan and Kofie are ready," I said as I noticed them approaching us.

"Wait a minute. You've got more of those? Let me hear a few real quick," Delaney whispered.

"Not now, love, I'll tell you later," I said as I gave him a seductive wink.

"Oh, now, I really like that one. Say that one again for me," Delaney flirted.

"I told you, honey, not now. Wait until some other time,"

"Oh, she's driving me crazy," Delaney said to Morgan and Kofie as they approached.

Delaney gave me a huge bear hug and I truly enjoyed his touch. He then looked at me, as if he didn't have a care in the world, as if everything around him didn't exist. Much like the way he looked at me earlier at the poetry reading.

"Damn. Let me stop. Alright. I'm okay now," Delaney said, shaking off as if he were trying to get himself together.

"He grabbed my hand this time and led me to the door. He squeezed it and I couldn't help but notice how warm, strong, and soft his hand was. Again, his touch made me tingle inside.

When we got outside, Morgan and I agreed to meet Delaney and Kofie at Ms. Tootsie's a soul food restaurant on South Street. Since Morgan and I came together, we made it a rule to always leave together.

One time I went to a club in Delaware with one of my European sisters, by the name of Diane, and after one too many drinks she decided that she was going home with an ex-boyfriend. Luckily for me I had driven my own car. After fuming all the way home, no sooner than I had taken a shower and said my prayers, Diane was calling me telling me how after I left the club, the ex-boyfriend changed all of a sudden and wanted her to go home with him and another girl he met that night at the club. Now you know what he wanted. Diane was so upset that she stormed out of the club to go home, soon realizing that she had not driven and that I had also left her. After hitchhiking, she finally got a ride from some girls that she knew from her tanning salon. When I told Morgan, she flipped.

"Serves the bitch right. You don't do that kinda crap to someone you're suppose to be cool with. When we roll together, we roll back home together. I don't care how fine that man is, he'll still be fine in the morning when you catch up with him the next day," Morgan said.

When we arrived at Ms. Tootsie's, the petite, black waitress who appeared to be in her late forties seated us in a booth in the back of the restaurant. She placed a menu in front of each of us and then hurried away to bring us each a glass of water.

Ms. Tootsie's is a Philadelphia tradition, known for its excellent soul food dinners and scrumptious desserts. I especially love the pound cakes and sweet potato pies, which are simply delectable. I usually hate taking those desserts home with me because they seem to call my name, which wasn't good for my thighs.

I knew that Morgan would want me to go in-line skating with her on Saturday, but she had another thing coming. She's like a drill sergeant at times. I don't know where she gets her stamina. Where we skate, it's nine miles around the Benjamin Franklin Parkway and sometimes Morgan wants to go twice, screaming at the top of her lungs, "Come on, faster, faster." I tell you it really drives me crazy, but I know that my body is always thankful.

"Hi, my name is Ms. Val and I'll be your waitress this evening. Would you all like to hear the day's specials?" Ms. Val asked.

Before we could answer, she started calling out the specials, which included suicide hot wings and fried potato cakes; deep-fried flounder and eggs; and waffles, bacon, sausage and eggs. Of course I wanted order something light, but I always want to everything fried. It's a habit I'm trying to outgrow. It's certainly not good for the arteries.

Delaney ordered the hot wings and potato cakes, I ordered a Cajun grilled chicken salad, Kofie ordered the flounder and eggs,

Only Fools Gamble Twice

and Morgan ordered waffles with a side order of fried potatoes. While we waited for the food to arrive, the four of us had light conversation about the upcoming boxing match between Victor Ramos and Alberto Casellas, which was a much-anticipated match showing on Pay-Per-View.

As it turned out Morgan and Delaney were hopeful about Ramos, and Kofie and I had our hopes on Casellas.

I was ordering the fight and was in the process of coordinating a small party at my town house.

"Don't forget, Tay, next week you'd better have my money," Morgan stated. We had actually bet fifty dollars on the upcoming fight.

"What's this fifty dollars all about?" Kofie asked.

"Oh no, Morgan seems to think she's going to earn fifty dollars from me for the fight next week. I'm having a small fight party at my house," I explained

"Wow, you ladies are serious fans. Buying the fight on Pay-Per-View and all. Sounds like it's going to be lots of fun," Kofie responded

"I completely forgot all about the fight next week," I said, placing my hand over my head.

"Oh, I see you ladies are high rollers. You don't meet too many women willing to place wagers on fights," Delaney replied with raised eyebrows.

"Just make sure you break me off with my ends. Thanks for the new sandals you just bought me," Morgan said as she winked at me.

"Yeah, yeah, yeah. We'll see next week. Just make sure you bring plenty of cash," I said as I threw my hands in the air.

I figured I would see how things turned out between Delaney and me, and if he was all that he seemed to be, I would invite him to next week's fight party.

When the food arrived, it was no surprise everything looked and smelled delicious. Delaney tried some of my Cajun chicken salad and I tried one of his suicidal hot wings, which almost burned my tongue off. After biting into the hot wing I had to instantly grab my water to cool my mouth, which caused Delaney, Kofie, and Morgan to all laugh.

"I don't know why you played yourself, Tay. You know that there are certain things that you can't eat, and yet you always push your luck and eat them anyway," Morgan said as she continued to laugh.

"Oh, shut up, Morgan. I know I can't eat hot foods but I think they're good anyway," I said as I pouted.

"Morgan, you better leave Taylor alone. She's dear to my heart now, and I make it a point to protect what's important to me," Delaney said jokingly, coming to my rescue, as he placed his large muscular arm around me.

"Yeah, that's right, Morgan. Stop teasing me before I hit you upside your head with one of Delaney's muscles," I said as we all laughed.

"Oh, no you won't, man. I like Morgan just as much and I just might have to cut you," Kofie said in his deep African accent. The four of us burst out laughing. We realized we were quite loud when the waitress cut her eye at us.

We continued to make jokes while we ate, but quietly. We didn't want to get kicked out. I hate when Black folks go out and are extremely loud, as if they haven't ever been anywhere.

Ms. Val appeared and asked if we wanted to order anything else. We all agreed that we were stuffed and Ms. Val placed the check in the middle of the table. Although I wanted to order a slice of pie, I thought better of it. It would be too hard to work off my thighs.

Delaney removed his arm from around me, which by the way, he kept around my shoulders, while he massaged the back of my neck--*whew,* and reached for the check. He looked it over and then said, "I got it, dinner is on me," in his deep baritone voice.

"Oh no man, let me help you with that check. At least let me pay for half," Kofie stated.

"Well how about if things work out, maybe we'll be fortunate enough to take these beautiful ladies out again, then dinner's on you," Delaney responded.

As I looked at Morgan, she gave me one of those looks of approval. A look that said she liked Delaney's style. As I looked at Delaney I thought, *This brother really has class.* I could get used to it all. The way he looked at me, the neck rubs, the way he carried himself, the way he spoke, his mannerisms, everything.

Delaney paid the check and left a substantial tip for Ms. Val. As we exited the restaurant, Delaney and I walked over to his SUV, holding hands.

"I really had a great time, Delaney. Let me ask you something. Do you have a nickname?" I asked, looking up at this big, strong handsome man with the beautiful smile and electrifying eyes.

"My boys call me Dee or Del, but I like the way you say my name," Delaney responded.

"I like saying your name, Delaney," I said softly, peering

into his jet-black eyes.

"I'd really like to thank you for the eats. That was really nice of you to treat all of us like that," I said as I looked up seriously at him. His skin resembled the color of an old penny.

"Please, Taylor, there is no need to thank me, although I appreciate your gratitude. If you really want to thank me, you'll invite me to that fight party of yours next week. Or better yet, you'll call me tomorrow so I can really get to know you better," Delaney said as he handed me his personal business card.

"Of course I'll call you. I had thought about inviting you to the party, but I wasn't sure of your personal situation at home," I said as I playfully nudged him in the side.

"First, I want you to call me at home tomorrow. That's my home number I gave you. I told you I'm not married so I don't have a hidden wife or even a secret girlfriend lurking around. I like you and I want to get to know you better. Like I said earlier, I'm tired of meeting senseless women who don't have a clue as to what they really want from a man. You really seem different, like we're on the same page," Delaney said seriously.

"I want you to call me tomorrow. A lot of so-called adults claim that they don't want to play games, will wait for a few days before they call. I really like you. You seem like you have so many things going for yourself and you appear to be somewhat interested in me. If I'm correct, we both like each other, then why should we play those dating games and wait three days before we see who'll call first? I mean as a man, I know if the fellas could hear me they would call me a fool and say that my player's card should be revoked right, " Delaney said jokingly.

"Oh, so you're a player, huh? I asked, becoming suddenly concerned.

"I'll put it to you like this, every man has been a player at least once in his life. Some of us are fifty years old and still hold on dearly to that card. Some brothers are twenty and turn in the card right away, the minute they meet that special lady. Some men will turn in the card, only to retrieve it later on down the line, and then you have some men, no matter what age they are, who will turn it in when they find that one woman who makes them never want to be a player ever again," Delaney said, looking directly into my eyes.

"Well, what kind of player are you?" I asked.

"Call me and find out," he said as he gently kissed me on my forehead with those soft, juicy lips and then turned and climbed into his SUV.

He started the car and then turned down the smooth sounds of Will Downing playing in the background. For a minute, I thought that he was going to leave me standing there without saying another word, but then he pushed the button for the automatic window and the window glided down. Delaney then said, "Can you handle that, Taylor? Can you put your faith in a man that you just met?" he questioned.

"Yeah, I can, Delaney. If the man is worth my trust. Are you a man that I can trust?" I asked.

"I think so, but then again I'm a little biased. Whenever you're getting to know someone, it's always a gamble," he replied. "I think you're a gamble I may be willing to take, but we'll talk about that later," I responded.

This time it was my turn to kiss him. I moved closer to his vehicle and placed a soft kiss on his cheek. My mother didn't raise no hoochie mama and I wasn't about to kiss some man I didn't know. "I promise I'll call you tomorrow. Once again thanks for the grub, and you have a safe ride home," I said as I turned to walk away.

It dawned on me that I knew very little about Delaney. I didn't know where he actually worked or where he lived. I know we talked about where he attended school and friends we had in common, but neither of us talked about where we lived. When I looked down at Delaney's business card, I realized he worked in Philadelphia, but he had a Delaware area code for his home number. This was a good sign. If Morgan had never seen him in Wilmington before, then it was a good possibility that he was really not a player. Like I said earlier, Morgan knows practically everyone in Delaware. I was pleased. With us living so close to each other, this would really give me an opportunity to really get to know him.

Morgan and Kofie were sitting in his car talking when Delaney drove off. Delaney beeped his horn and then Kofie beeped back as they waved good-bye. While I was sitting in Morgan's car I had time to think about Delaney as I popped in one of Morgan's CDs. The soft, sweet music and Jill Scott's butter-smooth voice totally relaxed me. I lay my head back as I listened to the words and thought of everything that happened that night. Delaney was definitely someone I wanted to get to know. Like I told him earlier, he seemed like he was worth the gamble. I knew on one hand I really didn't have many relationships to draw from experience, but on the other hand, like he said, "every relationship is a gamble." Maybe he wouldn't even be worth my time, but I was just going to have to call him to find out.

4/MORGAN

While Kofie and I sat in his car, he talked about his nighttime position as a drug rehabilitation specialist at drug treatment center, his job as a guidance counselor at Philadelphia's Community College, and his part ownership his family's African clothing store in New York.

"If you have all of these business ventures, how do you find time for yourself?" I asked.

"You see, it is really not my intention to have too much free time. I get to go out with some of my friends and coworkers from time to time, and that's what I did tonight. I make time for special things and special people when the time is right. I definitely didn't think I'd be out so late tonight. I didn't know I'd meet a beautiful lady, like yourself. I mean I am pleased that I did, but I am supposed to travel to New York tomorrow to see about my business," Kofie explained.

"Well, thank you for the compliment, but I guess I need to let you go. You have quite a long ride ahead of you tomorrow," I stated, feeling horrible because Kofie would be so tired on his drive to New York.

"No, please, I'm enjoying myself. I am a man who normally gets an average of five hours of sleep, sometimes less. I'll be fine. If I don't get there until the afternoon, that's fine. My brother-in-law doesn't need me to work. Im just going to help out in the store. I should let you go. Your friend is waiting for you," Kofie said.

"Yeah, I guess you're right. I'd better be going," I stated as I looked over at my car and noticed Taylor laid back with her eyes closed.

"Before I go, I don't believe I asked you if you were married with children, Kofie," I asked now becoming serious.

"Well, when I was twenty-two, I was still living in Cameroon, Africa. That is considered to be quite old in my country and not be married. My father was really pushing for me to get married to a young woman whose father owed my father a considerable amount of money. The man wanted to repay my father with his daughter's dowry. My father really wanted his payment, so he was eager for me to marry this woman. I didn't want to marry her and my father became very upset at me. I wanted to travel and see the world before I chose to become settled down with a family.

My older brother had been living in London for two years and when he visited, I asked him to take me back with him. I knew once I told my father that I refused to marry this woman he would be irate so I made arrangements to leave home before I explained my position to him. When I told my father, I got the response that I knew I would. To make a long story short, I was on the next plane to London and then six months later, I moved to the United States. I have not been home to see my family for twelve years. To answer your question, no I don't have a wife or any children," Kofie explained, and a look of sadness appeared on his face.

"That's so unfortunate, Kofie. Do you ever talk to your family?" I asked.

"Each month I talk to my older brother. My mother has forgiven me and understands that a person has to be happy with his life. My father is still upset and has subsequently disowned me as his son. My mother calls me about every three weeks to check on me and from time to time she'll send me care packages. I in turn send her things from the states every chance I get," Kofie explained with a look of discomfort on his face.

"Anyway, enough about me. I see that Taylor is waiting for you and I know that you have a long drive back to Delaware, so you better get going," Kofie said.

"Yeah, I guess we better get on the road. I had a great time, and thanks for the drinks and good conversation tonight," I said with a wide smile that I hoped would cheer him up. As I turned my back to open the car door I realized that Kofie and I had not exchanged phone numbers.

"I neglected to give you my phone number, Kofie. Here, let me find a business card in this bag of mine," I said as I rummaged through my handbag.

"Wait, do you have an answering machine at home?" Kofie asked.

"Yeah, what does that have to do with anything?" I asked, becoming confused.

"Okay, what is your phone number?" Kofie asked as he reached for his cellular phone.

"It's 302-555-2893," I responded. He dialed and I could hear my message pick up. When the signal sounded, Kofie left a message on my answering machine with his phone number. We then left my phone number in his voice mailbox.

"See, that way we don't have to bother with those business cards. I receive tons of them all the time, and half the time I have to write a short story on the back just to remember where I met the person and what happens if you misplace the business card?

Then the person that you gave the number to thinks that you're a liar when you tell them that you misplaced their number when you don't call initially," Kofie explained.

"Although that is a simple idea, I can't say that I would have ever thought of that, Kofie. Thanks for the tip. Now that I think of it, you can do the same thing with a beeper as well. Just put the phone number in and save the number and the piece of paper or business card is eliminated again," I said proudly.

"Now you got it," Kofie said, smiling for the first time in ten minutes.

"Alright, I'll talk to you later. I better get over there before Taylor slobbers on my leather seats. I know she's probably knocked out," I said as I climbed out of Kofie's two-door sports car.

As I walked the short distance across the parking lot to my car I thought the warm summer night felt great on my face. There's nothing like summer. You can give me ninety degrees any day and I would be happy. The hotter the weather the better things were for me.

When I reached my car, I turned around and waved to Kofie as he pulled off and waved good-bye. I climbed into my car and realized I was right, Taylor had indeed been slobbering on my leather seats.

"Wake your sleepy ass up, girl, and quit waxing my seats with that thick slime," I teased.

"Girl, if you wouldn't have left me in the car for an hour, I would have been awake. How could you leave me in the car all by myself? Someone could've car-jacked me. Where's the love for a sista?" Taylor asked rather dramatically.

Only Fools Gamble Twice

"Be quiet. Don't nobody want you. I mean damn, if a car jacker would have kidnapped you and then heard your whining, he would have paid me to take you back. Besides you know my dad is a captain of the police department. We got your back. Plus, you know I know a little Tae-Bo," I teased.

"Shut up and take me home so I can get up to go to church tomorrow," Taylor responded, as she laid her head back on the leather seat.

"Church? Taylor, tomorrow is Saturday, goof ball. Besides it's three-thirty in the morning and you're talking about you would go to church if tomorrow were Sunday?" I asked in disbelief.

"Well, you know what I mean, I meant to say work. Besides, if it were Sunday then I would still be getting up early to go to church. It wouldn't matter if it was 3:30. That's the problem with you heathen folk, you can get up in the morning and go make that dollar for the man, but talk about church on a Sunday morning and y'all talk about y'all tired. Girl, tired or not, I'm going to work tomorrow and then Sunday I'm getting up and going to praise the Lord," Taylor said, as she threw her hands in the air.

That shit really got me pissed. I'm okay to hang out in the streets to get down and dirty with, but then Taylor up and flips the script on me. I ain't one for throwing stuff up in somebody's face, but just a few months ago I asked Taylor if she wanted to go to a birthday party with me and she told me I needed to stop dancing for the devil. Now she's all up in my face talking about I'm a heathen. It's all good though. I know her kind any day of the week. You see church is wonderful when her life is not going as fantastic as she'd like it--i.e., she doesn't have a man. As soon as she gets a man, church won't be good enough for her. Mark my words. I'm not saying another thing. I've seen it too many times in the past. Watch all the other things about her change too. First sex, then the language, and all bets will surely be off. Just watch. Y'all don't hear me though. Can I get an amen?

Every Sunday, Taylor attended church, all the way in Philly with her mom, Ms. Barbara. Following church, Taylor's mom would fix a huge soul food type of meal, which was always slamming. Ms. Barb turned to the church when her husband died a few years ago. From what Taylor tells me, Ms. Barb used to be built like a brick house, but after all of her problems she encountered with drugs and alcohol, her body looked as if had seen better days. But I'm not one to gossip so I'm gonna let Taylor tell it. Ms. Barb can, however, throw down in those pots. She makes some awesome peach cobbler. Now that her mom has become a born-again Christian and dedicated her life to the Lord she expects her daughter to walk in her foot steps, so to speak. But, quiet as it's kept, I know Ms. Barb still has a little wild side to her. You can just see it in her eyes. See, you all are trying to make me gossip up in here.

"To answer your original question, I do have to stop by the office in the morning, and then my church is having a backyard cookout. So why don't you get up early and go with me and after the cookout we can go skating?" Taylor said.

"I don't think so. I'm sleeping in late tomorrow. I don't want to do anything but sleep, sleep, sleep. I've had one hell of a week and I just want to rest. I need to find some time to clean up my dirty-ass house. Anyway, I wouldn't want the church grounds to burn up when I walk on them with my hot, sinning feet. Look at it as if I'm saving the church from destruction," I said jokingly.

"Not funny. God loves us for who we are and doesn't care about what we've done, only that we come to him for guidance," Taylor responded as she continued to lay back in the comfort of the seats as I headed for I-95 South to Delaware.

"Maybe some other time," I said softly. "Just know that at my church, we make it a point not to judge others. There's a lot of people who are strung out on drugs and everything, but my pastor believes that as long as you come and try to be the best Christian you can, who is he to turn His back on you when the Lord never turns his back on you? Each week, my pastor feeds the homeless and the disadvantaged without asking anything from them. Most of the time, he just wants them to know that he's a messenger from the Lord and that he's there for them when they need him," Taylor proclaimed proudly.

"When I'm ready to go to church, you will be the first to know, Reverend Taylor," I responded.

To me, it seemed as if I were on the attack. I couldn't hold it back any longer. I had to know. "Let me ask you this, why are you still out here in these clubs then if you're such a devout Christian? Remember, you asked me a few months ago why I was in the clubs, still dancing for the devil? Now here you are. Right along with me. There's nothing in these clubs for you," I said.

"Don't judge me! Don't you dare judge me! I have asked for deliverance. I continue to pray on it and ask God to deliver me from temptation. Just remember, there's no such thing as a perfect person," Taylor responded, rather angrily.

"First of all, slow your roll. Secondly, I would never judge you, but you sure find a way to want to judge me. How easily you forget how you questioned me about my lifestyle, but remember that I would never question you like that. I also know that you can't serve two masters. Just because I don't go to church each and every week like you doesn't make you any less worldly than me. Don't dish it out if you can't take it, " I replied, now becoming extremely irritated.

Taylor said nothing. She just closed her eyes and acted as if she was asleep, but I knew she wasn't. She knew I was right. I love Tay like a little sister, but she could be a bit self-righteous at times. Fornicating on Saturday and jumping, clapping, and praising the Lord on Sunday. Although she says she's not being judgmental, I see it a little differently. I knew her when. But I'm not one to judge. I have my own issues I'm dealing with about church, not necessarily with the church, but the people who're in it.

I've never told Taylor why I won't attend church with her; I just avoid the topic at all costs. It's not that I am totally against church, it's just that when I was eighteen, I was really involved in the church where I had grown up and attended my whole life. Our pastor, Reverend Simpson, retired and we entrusted Reverend Atkins, a middle-aged man who had been a member for quite a long time, with the church. Reverend Atkins was a deacon in the church before he became a reverend. The summer before I attended Delaware State University, I would type the church announcements when the church secretary needed my assistance. One Saturday evening, Reverend Atkins asked me to stay after the service to take dictations for his sermon for the following morning. Since I usually just typed the announcements, I had to find a handheld tape recorder. Although I had plans that evening, I agreed and told Reverend Atkins that I would meet him in his office after I made a call to postpone my plans. After I made the phone call I realized that I had a recorder in my pocketbook from the choir rehearsal we had earlier. I then walked upstairs to Reverend Atkins' office. I heard gospel music on the radio in his office and thought I better knock. When I opened the door Reverend Atkins was not in the room. I called out to him and he told me to have a seat.

"I'll be right out, Sister Morgan. I'm in the bathroom. Have a seat and I'll be with you in a minute."

I was listening to the gospel music, eyes closed, and rather caught up in the word. About thirty seconds later, I felt a presence in front of me and when I opened my eyes Reverend Atkins was standing directly in front of me butt naked. Before I knew it, Reverend Atkins was rubbing himself telling me how badly he wanted me. After I came out of shock and realized what was happening before my very eyes, I decided right then and there that the reverend needed to be taught a valuable lesson. Now, don't get me wrong, I've never been the shy, innocent type and wouldn't have professed to be then or now, but I know when a grown man ought to stay in a grown man's place. Like I said, my Dad is a police officer and he taught me a thing or two about the streets.

"So, I guess my secret is out, huh?" I stated in my best seductive voice.

"Huh? I mean yeah. Morgan, I know you want me. My wife told me how she doesn't like the way you look at me. She says that you look like you're hot in the ass," Reverend Atkins replied confidently.

"You know what? Your wife is right, I am hot in the ass,

and only you can put out the fire that's in me." At this point I figured that my place was marked in hell and that I might as well have some fun with it. I know that vengeance is the Lord's, but I just couldn't let this asshole get away with this. The way I figured it was who would believe me? I knew my parents would, but I just didn't want murder to be the outcome. My parents taught me how to defend myself in these types of situations, so that's what I was planning to do.

    I stood and then began unbuttoning my dress, taking one step closer toward Reverend Atkins. I was so close that I could see the tiny beads of sweat forming on his fat, bald head and I could smell his horrific bad breath. I don't know where I was getting this nerve. Not only was I not hot in the ass as the reverend stated, but I was the only eighteen-year-old virgin that I knew, including all of the girls attending the church. Yeah, I was tough and didn't take any shit from anybody, but I was also just a simple girl who minded her own business and didn't bother anyone.

    "I want you to get on your knees and suck my dick like it's the last dick you'll ever see," Reverend Atkins boldly stated.

    His nasty fat ass stomach was pushing up against me. I almost choked on the vomit that was slowly climbing up my throat. I wish I could have seen the look on my face because I'm sure I had to be looking quite disgusted. I assume it didn't bother Big Daddy Fat Ass because he kept on pursuing.

    "Okay, Daddy, I'm gonna give it to you like nobody ever gave it to you before, but before I do I want you to sit down so I can give it to you good," I stated seductively. I started kissing on his legs. I then spread his legs open wide.

The stench that came from his balls almost paralyzed me. I held my breath and placed my mouth over his penis. I had never given anyone oral sex, but from the moans coming from Reverend Atkins' mouth, I would say that I wasn't doing too badly. Just when I was giving it to him good, I took his penis in my mouth for the last time. I thought the man was going to explode right then and there. As I was pulling his penis out of my mouth, I bit down so hard that I drew blood and a nice chunk of his dick to boot.

"Ouch! Oh, Lord! Save me! You stinkin' bitch! I can't believe you did that to me!" the reverend cried in utter pain, as he looked totally bewildered.

I then walked over and slapped Reverend Atkins so hard, I knew that his wife and kids felt it.

"Now you go home and tell your wife how you lost a chunk of meat from your fat, funky dick! And for the record, I want you out of this church, and if I ever see you again I will have your black ass arrested for rape," I stated angrily.

"Rape? Girl, you're crazy. It's just your word against mine. Who do you really think is going to believe you over a man of the cloth?" the reverend stated arrogantly as he held his bleeding penis. "You're right, reverend, who would believe me? But you see I just happen to have this recorder in my pocketbook and I taped everything that just transpired, so if you don't want to be some prisoner's bitch, I suggest you do as you're told," I responded coolly.

Of course the recorder was never on, but he didn't know that and I don't think he wanted to chance it. In the next move, I gathered my belongings and headed for the door. As I did so, I quickly turned on my heel and stated ever so calmly, "Oh yeah, Rev, I don't know if you know this or not but my family has a long line of law enforcement officers. My daddy is a captain with the Wilmington Police Department, and his two brothers are Delaware State Troopers. If you start to catch amnesia, I suggest you do it elsewhere because you might find yourself preachin' at your own funeral." With that statement I headed out the door and haven't stepped foot in another church.

My parents were never really big churchgoers anyway, just figured that I grew out of the church and they never tried to get me to go back. Of course I attend weddings and funerals, but that's all I'm willing to do now. I still believe in God and I pray faithfully and read my Bible, but I just can't seem to get back to church.

I know that not all men of the cloth are not bad people, hell my great-grandfather was a reverend, but I am just not ready to go back to church just yet. Too many painful memories. I never did tell my mom and dad, or anyone for that matter, what happened that night, I just made excuses for the rest of that summer before I went to school and then when I graduated from DSU, I moved into my own apartment.

"Will you please slow down?" Taylor hollered, interrupting my thoughts.

"Oh, my bad. I didn't know I was going that fast," I responded.

"I don't want to fight about church. We both have our issues, and we're both dealing with them. Just let me know if you ever want to go to church with me. I just hope it's before my wedding to Delaney," Taylor said.

Only Fools Gamble Twice

"What do you mean your wedding to Delaney? Slow your roll, girlfriend. You just met him tonight. You don't even know anything about him yet," I replied as I brought the odometer down from eighty-five miles per hour to the legal limit of sixty-five.

"So you never told me what you think of my future husband, Delaney," Taylor said, completely ignoring my statement about not knowing anything about him.

"He seems like a really down-to-earth brother. It's not too many guys you meet these days who not only want to pay for a sister's meal that he just met, let alone her friend and one of his boys too. Yeah, Mr. Delaney seems as if he has class, and he's not bad-looking either. However, you don't know anything about him. Take your time," I responded.

"Yeah, he is fine and definitely a true gentleman. And for your information, we talked all night and I feel as if I've known him for an eternity already," Taylor stated dreamily.

"Slow down, girl. They're all good in the beginning. You have to do a background check on these brothas. You have to find out if he has a baby's mama or not."

"No, he doesn't have any kids," Tay replied.

"Well a lot of men will tell you anything. You know my peeps can run a check on the guy if you want. 'Cause don't even think I'm not going to have Mr. Kofie checked out thoroughly," I stated.

"Can't they get in trouble for that?" Tay asked coyly.

"Please, my dad is the man. I don't think anyone is going to question him. It doesn't hurt to make sure you're not dealing with some sort of psychopath, you know what I mean,"

I stated. "So what do you think of Kofie," I asked carefully.

"He came across as a nice person. To be honest though, he seems like he's a little domineering," Tay said.

"I know. I have to make sure that I check him in the future because ain't no man going to be running me. I ain't having that Umfufu shit with some damn bone in my nose sitting on some horse butt naked," I stated matter of factly.

"Well, just be careful, because I told you about my aunt's husband," Tay said.

"Yeah, you told me. Did she ever find out what happened to that bum?" I asked.

"He just up and left, never to be heard from again. It's like he disappeared off the face of the earth," Tay said, becoming a little sad.

Taylor's aunt Cheryl was in her mid-thirties when she met and married this guy from goodness knows where. The whole family despised him because of the controlling way he talked to her, but she was adamant about the way she felt about him. It just so happened that Tay's aunt Cheryl had never married and desperately wanted to have children, before it was too late. On their one-year anniversary she came home from work to find that all his belongings were removed from the house, with not even so much as a note saying that he left her. She found all of her jewelry and the ten thousand dollars that they shared in a joint savings account gone too.

"Don't worry, Tay, I'll be careful. Now do you see why I think it's important to have people checked out?" I asked.

"Does that mean you had me checked out too?" Tay asked jokingly.

"Yup, you bet. I had to make sure you weren't some crazy

and deranged lunatic," I teased.

Tay and I continued to joke on the ride home and then I dropped her off, making sure she was safely in the house and then I headed to my crib. I wasn't worried because I'm always strapped. I've never told Tay because I know she would be way too worried, but it's just me living on my own. I have to protect myself. Mommy and Daddy live on the other side of town, way too far to help me if someone's on my ass.

When I got home, I called Tay to let her know that I had gotten in safely. This was a rule we insisted on following when we went out. Sometimes I would forget and Tay would call and curse me out and tell me how inconsiderate I was for having her worry. Tay was such a woman, although sometimes I thought she took her role too seriously. As much as she complained about her mother mandating her to call, she did the same thing to me. It was like we balanced each other. She kept me in check and I tried like hell to do the same. After all, Tay had no family in Delaware, except me that is, so I felt obligated to watch her back, just like a big sister. As soon as I could, I was going to talk her into getting a little heater for herself. She damned sure needed it in that townhouse. An alarm doesn't do anything if someone's runnin' up on you. It takes the alarm forty-five seconds to go off before the alarm company even calls you to find out if you're dead or alive. My heater keeps me safe and warm. Screw that old ass alarm system.

I took a shower, turned on the TV, and then noticed the light flashing on my answering machine. For a minute I forgot that Kofie had left his number so I ran for a pen only to hear that the first three messages were from Mister.

"Morgan, this is Mister. Baby, pick up the phone, I know you're there. I miss you and I can't stand to be without you," there was a long pause. "Okay, I see you're playing hardball. I'll talk to you later."

Next message. "Come on Morgie, pick-up the phone...alright damn, you know what I ain't gonna sweat you forever. You know we're good for each other." Next message.

"Morg, babe, pick up the phone, I need to talk to you and I don't want to do it over the phone. All right you pushed me to it. Don't call me anymore. Be stupid, why don't you? That's all right, 'cause I'm moving on anyway. Peace out!" Mister yelled.

Before he hung up, there was a long pause then. " I shouldn't have said that. Call me girl. I still love you."

Love me? How in the hell could he even say that? Mister didn't know the meaning of love. He had all types of the frustration bottled inside of him. I think he was a victim, like so many other young brothers. Being a single black man growing up in this world without a strong black father in his life led him to not trust many people. Mister's father was there in the beginning, but then he abandoned his mother and younger brother, which forced Mister to be the man of the family. Although a good man, he was very confused and frustrated. Deep down inside I think he cares greatly for me but he has issues he needs to work out for himself first.

I had to realize that I couldn't heal Mister by being his rock. I guess being with me was a constant reminder just how weak he was as a man. I am a constant reminder of his failures.

The next message was from my line sister, Carla. Apparently, she was a little upset that I still hadn't made it to her

Only Fools Gamble Twice

club, the Butter Cup Lounge. I was going to get there. She just needed to be a little patient with a sista. I would send her a dessert basket to celebrate the new business and get over there ASAP before she killed me for real. The next message was from Kofie. I jotted his phone number down on a piece of paper and also saved the message just in case I lost the phone number. Although Kofie was apparently a little domineering, I liked his character. There are not too many men or women out there in this world who like to work hard for what they have. Kofie was different. Besides who wants somebody who is like everyone else? Not me. If Kofie was about something positive, then I at least owed a chance at getting to know him. I wanted to get to know him a little better before I passed judgment on the brother. I did however have to make sure the brother's on the up and up. I have a friend from Nigeria who attended DSU that I was going to question about Kofie. One thing about the African American community, no matter if you live in New Jersey, Philadelphia, or Delaware, somebody knew someone who would know Kofie. I had to make sure he was on the up and up. My friend Ngecho is very adamant about making sure the African brothers maintain a high moral character here in the states. If anyone knew the skinny on Kofie, Ngecho could tell me. I just had to remind myself to reach out to him.

    It's a shame that my trust level for men is at an all-time low. But just because Mister had acted like an asshole to me, not communicating his feelings, that didn't mean that all men were that way. Besides, no one said that Kofie and I would become an item. He's just another person to add to the many people that I know. The way I meet people, this was no big deal. Just another brother who had to prove he was worthy of my time and attention.

    I drew a bath, turned on my Bilal CD, and slowly began to relax. Today was a good day. I finally felt that Mister was out of my life and I could begin to see the light at the end of the proverbial tunnel. Yes, life was good.

5/TAYLOR

I don't need an alarm clock in the morning to wake me up. Between Gerald and Eddie, my two parakeets making that screeching noise, and Lacey, my cat who thinks she's a person, jumping on my stomach and making that purring noise in my ear, who could sleep? Sometimes, I think they talk to one another when I'm not at home to synchronize their internal alarm clocks just to get me up and running.

I got out of bed, showered, fed Lacey, fed the birds, fixed some coffee, got dressed, and was out the door, headed for work. I needed to install four programs on several laptops before Monday. It's not like I had to go to work, it's just that I wanted to get a jumpstart on Monday's schedule. Like I said, being a young minority, I feel all sorts of pressure and I want to stay on top of my game.

After installing the programs, I checked my watch and was right on schedule. The church cookout started at one and it was now noon.

I jumped in my car for the thirty-five minute drive to Philadelphia to make it to FDR Park in South Philly, where the cookout was being held.

When I arrived, I greeted several of the church members, kissed all of the babies, and said hello to the elderly. I saw my mom, waved her down, and headed toward her and the church ladies with whom she was undoubtedly gossiping.

Knowing Mom and the ladies they were talking about all of the happenings over the past week, in and around the church-- what member never hit the right note in the church choir or who was trying to get brownie points with the pastor.

"Good afternoon, Mom. Good afternoon, Ms. Burton, Mrs. James," I said as I planted a kiss on my mom.

My mother is a very attractive woman. She's finally picked up some weight after all of the years of being skinny from the drugs and alcohol. At forty-nine, she's still got it goin' on. I'm just so glad to have her off the drugs and now dedicating her life to the Lord.

My mom is a bank teller at one of the largest African-American-owned banks in downtown Philadelphia. She continues to work hard to maintain the house and support herself and my younger brother Malik. My mother stopped supporting my brother Tyrone when he turned eighteen, because she said she wasn't taking care of a grown man. That got Ty off his butt and enrolled in a community college. He then got a part-time job so my mother started helping him when he really needed something. She still makes him pay rent from time to time.

"Hey, Tay. I thought you were going to stop by and pick up Malik?" Mom said.

"I called from work and he said he didn't want to come. He said something about going to the mall with his friends," I explained.

"I'll be glad when he gets out of this stage. All he wants to do is play that stupid video game, talk on the phone, and hang out with his friends. But at least he's not getting into any trouble. Lord knows it's hard to raise boys these days," Mom said to no one in particular.

"Tay, you still not married, baby? You know my son, Hakeem, just got out of Gratersford and he could sure use a good woman like yourself to keep him on track," Mrs. James said with a hopeful look.

"Gratersford? You mean as in the prison. I don't think so! My baby has a lot going for herself. By the way doesn't your son have six kids?" Mom questioned.

"Yeah, but he thinks the last two aren't his. As soon as he gets out of the halfway house, I'm marching him straight down there to get one of those tests I've seen on Montell or one of those other talk shows," Mrs. James replied very matter of factly.

I knew Mrs. James' son, Michael, very well. The brother went to prison and now called himself Hakeem. Michael used to always push up on me when we were younger. Always trying to feel me up in elementary school. I knew he was going to be trouble then. He had his first baby in the eighth grade. I'm not one to turn up my nose up on folks, but his nickname was Bad News. Why his mother always tried to push him off on me was a me. I don't think so. With his baby mama drama–having behind.

I stayed at the cookout with my mom until five o'clock. By that time, I had seen enough children and church folk to last a lifetime. I was supposed to call Morgan to go skating, but I just wasn't up for it. After getting in late the night before and then getting up early, I was seriously in need of a nap. I decided to head home and do just that.

By the time I arrived home, I did my ritual of feeding my cat and birds, taking a shower, and getting my tired bones in the bed. I must have been more tired than I had known, because I woke up at nine o'clock to the phone ringing.

"Hello, may I please speak with Taylor?" a strong male voice asked.

"This is Taylor," I responded, trying to get my bearings.

"It's Delaney. How are you doing? Were you asleep?" Delaney asked.

"Yeah, but I'm up now. I'm doing well. I figured I would take a nap earlier but I hadn't realized how tired I was," I responded, sitting up in bed, now recognizing how sexy his voice sounded over the phone.

"Sorry I'm calling so late. I figured you weren't going to be home on a Saturday night but I see I've got you live and direct," Delaney stated.

"I had to get up early and do a few things at work and then I went to a cookout. By the time I got home, all I could do was crash. I was going to call you when I got up, but who knew that I would sleep this late? I guess I needed the rest. I keep telling everyone I'm not as young as I used to be," I replied, still trying to wake up.

"Well, I didn't mean to wake you. I drove down to the shore earlier, a few of my coworkers have a house down there and they were having a cookout. I just got back home about an hour ago. I was planning on leaving you a really nice message," Delaney said seductively.

"Well now I'm upset that I picked up the phone. How about I hang up and you call me again? I'm a sucker for really nice messages," I replied, picturing Delaney in a pair of shorts, with no shirt and his muscles rippling as he sat in his bed talking to me.

"Naw, that's all right. I'd much rather talk to you than talk to your voicemail," Delaney responded.

Delaney and I talked for what seemed like hours.

Actually it was 2:30 A.M. when we finally decided to call it a night. We talked about everything. I even found out that he grew up in Philly, moved to Delaware about the same time that I had moved here, but still worked in Philly. We also talked about our goals and aspirations, marriage and politics.

I knew that Delaney was a computer programmer, but learned that he wanted to start his own consulting firm in another three years. I was amazed, because I had been tossing the idea around myself. We even talked about the possibility of starting our own business together one day. To say that I was truly impressed was the understatement of the year.

The next morning, I awakened to the animal house's normal routine. The birds were chirping nonstop and Lacey in normal form was, on my stomach purring in my face. I fed the rude animals and began my normal Sunday routine to get ready for church.

When I arrived, my mom and the church ladies were standing around talking and since I had been up so late, I didn't feel much like socializing.

Reverend Bradley preached a powerful sermon about loving one another and turning your problems over to the Lord and letting him keep those problems. The service was so powerful that most of the members in the audience were crying, and I even had to cry a few times. I started thinking about my relationship with my boss and how she totally stressed me out at work and how, although I had prayed about the subject, I kept reclaiming it.

"How you gonna ask the Lord to handle your problem, but yet you are constantly meddling in His business? Y'all don't hear me though. Turn it over to the Lord and let Him keep it!" proclaimed Reverend Bradley as he jumped up and down in the pulpit to make his point.

Reverend Bradley filled his sermon with how sometimes we stress ourselves out about what we're going to say and lose hours of sleep wondering about what we're going to do yet the Lord has it all figured out for us already.

"You stay up till the wee hours of the morning, worrying, crying, complaining, because you want your problem solved. But the Lord says, 'Trust in me and I'll fulfill all of your dreams. Trust Him! Turn it over to Him! Praise the Lord! Hallelujah," Reverend Bradley shouted as he ran back and forth across the front of the pulpit.

The sermon seemed to be in line with everything that I had been thinking. As the service came to a close, I couldn't help but feel refreshed and ready to turn all of my problems over to the Lord and let them stay there, once and for all.

After service, Mom and I talked to Reverend Bradley and some other members of the congregation for a while and then we headed to my mom's house for Sunday dinner.

"I'll meet you at the house, Mom. I have to make a stop at the ATM first," I said.

"All right, baby, now you hurry up. If you get there before me, make sure you reheat the greens and put the roast beef in the oven," my mom said enthusiastically as she turned back to her church friends to continue talking.

Knowing Mom and the church sisters they would be there for another hour or so, talking about the sermon and probably gossiping.

Only Fools Gamble Twice

I drove to the ATM to get some cash for the rest of the week and provide my mom with some extra cash for her and the boys. Since I was in such a great mood, I bought my mom a card. I carefully placed a fifty-dollar bill inside and signed the card:

> Love your favorite daughter, Taylor.
> P.S. I almost forgot, I'm your only daughter, so I guess I'm your favorite anyway.

Although my mom did alright financially, I tried to give her money whenever I had a little extra. Although my mom wouldn't take it, I had my ways of ensuring she got it. Sometimes I would take one of her utility bills home with me and all of a sudden the bill would be paid. Other times I would just put the money in my mom's purse. By the time she had realized that the money was in there, I'd be long gone. I decided I would put the envelope under my mom's pillow, knowing that Sunday nights she stripped her sheets and she would definitely find it by the time I had returned to Delaware. I think she sometimes felt guilty after all of the turmoil she'd put me through in the past.

My mom beat me to the house and when I arrived, I walked inside and was met with the aroma of collard greens, baked macaroni and cheese, pot roast, and sweet potato pie.

"Whew, it smells good in here. When did you have time to cook all of this, Mom?" I asked as I washed my hands in the kitchen sink so I could steal a taste of the food.

"I cooked my greens Friday night after work, and I got up early this morning and put my roast on, I bought the shredded cheese and I boiled the sweet potatoes last night. Dinner should be ready soon. Your brother Malik is around the corner playing football and Tyrone is over his girlfriend's house. So I guess it's just you and me for dinner. Is that all right?" my mom asked.

"Now you know it is. I'd rather not have those two loudmouths in here anyway. They would probably have that TV on making all of that noise with those video games and what not. And to be honest, that's more food for us. You know those boys can eat someone out of house and home," I joked. I excused myself and ran upstairs to place the envelope under Mom's pillow before I forgot. I then hurried back downstairs to join Mom in the kitchen.

"So did you have fun at the poetry reading Friday night with Morgan?"

"Yeah. We had a great time."

"I'm glad to see you two got in safely. I don't like you going home to an empty house in the middle of the morning. I can't understand why you and Morgan can't sleep over each other's house when you go out. Make me worry half to death," Mom rambled.

"Mom, I'm fine. Besides, I have Lacey at home to protect the crib when I'm not there. If anyone tries to break in, she'll rip their eyes out. Plus, you know I get my Tae-Bo on faithfully. Let somebody just try something. I'm looking to break somebody down," I said, proudly assumed a karate position.

"Now you know darn well that cat ain't ripping up nothing, except for a can of cat food. That cat is so lazy, he would probably get up, open the door for a robber, and then go back to sleep. And as far as *you're* concerned, you're talking about some Tae-Bo, chile, you need to put some meat on those bones. What you trying to lose weight for anyway? Don't no man want no bony woman," Mom teased.

"Well I guess some man does want some bony woman, because I guess I should tell you that I met my future husband last night," I said cautiously.

"Oh, really, and just what is my future son-in-law's name?" Mom replied.

"His name is Delaney. He's a computer programmer, single, no kids, lives in Delaware, works here in downtown Philly and so far he seems really nice. After we went to the poetry reading Friday night, we all went out to eat, and he not only treated me to breakfast, but he treated Morgan and one of his friends that was with us too," I explained.

I dared not tell Mom that I went to a club afterward. I would never hear the end of it. Every since Mom got off the drugs and became saved, she's a holy roller. I can handle it. I just don't want to disappoint her. My two brothers don't go to church with her and I know me going wither her is all she has now. So although I've never told Morgan, I'm really not ready to be as involved in the church as I am, I do it for my mom. I know it's not right, but who am I hurting really? I'm getting the word and I'm living the way the Lord wants me to live. I guess Mom doesn't want me to get involved in the lifestyle she lived for so long.

"You mean to tell me you and Morgan went out to breakfast until the wee hours of the morning with two men you just met? They could be serial killers for all you two know. That is not very ladylike, Tay. I thought I raised you better than that. That is not of God!" Mom said, disapprovingly.

"Mom, you act like I can't hold my own. For one thing Morgan and I drove in separate cars from Delaney and Kofie, and we all met in a very public place. I'd hardly think serial killers work in that kind of way," I replied, becoming a little irritated. "Alright, I guess I do allow my imagination to run a little wild. It's just that I worry about you, baby. You're my only daughter and if anything ever happened to you, I don't know what I'd do. I don't mean to worry so much, but I guess I do need to trust your judgment. But I just think you need to watch your walk. By the way, where do these people get these names from?" Mom questioned.

"I guess the same place you got my name from. You don't like his name?" I asked.

"Honey, if you like it, I love it. I just don't understand these crazy names. It seems like people just try to come up with something crazy. Just be careful with what's-his-name. You still don't know him," Mom rambled.

"Whatever, Mom. Now when can we eat?" I said as I put the matter behind us.

I knew that I had to watch what I told my mom. Last year I went on a business trip in Phoenix and I had met up with a girl who I knew from another office. We decided to rent a car and go sightseeing, then out to dinner. I had been gone all day and since there is a three-hour time difference between Philly and Phoenix, it was ten o'clock in Philly, but only seven o'clock in Phoenix. I had talked to my mom earlier in the day and told her of my plans. When my mom hadn't talked to me all day she began to worry. She called the hotel and demanded they send a state trooper out to find me. She left three messages for me at the front desk. When I arrived back to the hotel, the front desk clerk advised me to call my mother immediately. Initially I became concerned, so I hurried to call home. My mom picked up on the first ring.

"Tay, is that you?" Mom cried into the receiver.

"Yes, Mom, it's me. What's wrong?" I replied, thinking something had happened to one of my brothers.

"Where have you been? I was worried sick about you. I've been calling all over looking for you." Mom continued to cry.

"I told you I was going out. What's wrong with you?" I asked, becoming irritated.

"I don't know. I just started worrying. When you didn't call all day, I thought something bad happened to you," Mom replied, beginning to calm down.

"What on earth did you think happened to me?" I asked my mother, now beginning to calm down myself. As I sat down on the bed, Mom explained how she allowed her imagination to run wild.

It seems that Mom thought that I had gone out sightseeing only to have probably fallen off a cliff and then a coyote had eaten me alive. When I explained to her that I was with a friend, Mom thought that as my friend watched me fall over the cliff, she, too, fell and that we were both down there with no one to help us. That's why she explained that she wanted the Arizona State Police Department to put out an all points bulletin on me. After hearing her story, the only thing I could do was laugh.

I explained to my mother that she needed to stop allowing her imagination to run wild. She was okay for a while but when I went to New York a few months later for my birthday, the same thing happened all over again. Only this time, my mom called the CIA, and all of the other the federal agencies she could think of: Pennsylvania State Police, Delaware State Police, New York State Police and half of my coworkers and friends. By the time I arrived to work the following Monday, everyone had heard about this latest episode. To say that I was embarrassed is an understatement.

After eating, I stayed at my mom's for a while and finally both my brothers came strolling in. After talking to them for a brief moment and giving them my weekly lecture about not getting on Mom's nerves and to also remind them to help her out a little more around the house, I decided to head home. I said my good-byes and promised my mother that I'd call her the minute I arrived home. Of course she packed me several plates of food so that I wouldn't have to cook for the rest of the week. I was going to put some damage on that food and that pie. My thighs would forever hate me but you only live once.

As I made my way to I-95 South, I couldn't help but to think of Delaney. He had been on my mind all day. Delaney was a man who could probably make me fall and fall hard for that thing called love. I decided that I was definitely not going to play games, so I rummaged through my handbag to find my cellular phone and the paper with his phone number on it. When I arrived at a stop light, I carefully dialed his phone number. A man answered on the third ring.

"Braxton speaking," the man on the telephone line said.

I remembered that Delaney said he had moved in with his college roommate after he moved to Delaware.

"Hi, this is Taylor. May I please speak to Delaney?" I asked. "Braxton, man, I got it." Delaney's deep voice answered as I heard Braxton hang up on the other line.

"Hey, you, I am so glad you called. You must have ESP, because I was just laying here thinking about that beautiful smile of yours. I don't want to sound like a nut or anything or that I'm hard up, but lady, I sure do miss you already," Delaney said in a sexy voice.

"Well, I see you sure know how to make a sista blush. And by the way, your smile is all I could think of myself. In fact, I wanted to know if you wanted to get together soon," I responded.

"Just name the time and the place and I'll be there," Delaney said enthusiastically.

"What are you doing tonight?" I asked.

"Waiting for you to tell me where you want to meet."

"Well, what about your place?" I responded.

"My roommate, Braxton, is expecting company in about twenty minutes, so here is not where I want to be. You know if three is a crowd then four is probably a gang. How about grabbing something to eat? Where are you?" Delaney asked.

"I just came from my mom's house and I ate over there. I don't usually allow strange men to visit my home just after one day of meeting them, but I guess since we talked to the wee hours of the morning that qualifies us as long-lost friends. How about my place? Besides, after all, Morgan did meet you and knowing her she probably had you checked out already," I teased.

"Checked out? What do you mean?" Delaney asked.

"Well, Morgan is a bit on the paranoid side. I mean I guess in some instances it's good. Her father is a captain of the police department and she has just about everyone she comes in contact with checked out," I explained.

"Well, don't worry, my arrest record is clear now that I killed off my probation officer, so I think everything is going to be all right," Delaney teased. "Are you sure coming over to your place won't be a problem?" Delaney asked.

"Not a problem at all," I responded.

I gave Delaney the directions to my house and told him to give me about an hour so I could straighten up. Delaney said that he, too, had eaten already and since I had as well, he would bring some DVDs and some ice cream for our entertainment and pleasure.

I arrived home, took a quick shower, washed my hair, and fed the members of the wild kingdom. I put on my all-time favorite love song Stevie Wonder CD, listening over and over to "Ribbon in the Sky." I put on my much-loved pear-scented shower mist and began to straighten up my messy house. I let my hair air dry again, pulling it up in a ponytail, and put on a comfortable pink cotton dress.

Before Delaney arrived I called my mom to let her know that I had gotten in safely, and I told her I was just going to sit back and relax and have a quiet evening, not really a lie.

Normally, I would have told my mom my plans, but since our earlier conversation, I didn't want her to worry unnecessarily or call her friends at the local state police. Mom had actually grown a rapport with the guys at the police department.

When the doorbell rang at six-thirty, Lacey instantly sprang up from her cat nap and ran to the door. Sometimes she became confused and thought she was a dog. I scooped her up and ran her upstairs to the guest bedroom. I first wanted to see if

Delaney liked cats or if he was allergic.
    The doorbell rang a second time and I ran downstairs to answer the door. When I opened it Delaney was standing in the doorway looking very sensuous in a pair of blue jeans, a black cotton T-shirt, and a pair of black loafers.
    "Hey, gorgeous. You look good and smell even better," Delaney said as he flashed that wonderful smile of his, giving me a kiss on the cheek.
    "Why thank you, sir. Why don't you come on in?" I responded as I invited him into my home.
    "Before I do, I would like you to have these," Delaney said as he extended a bouquet of flowers and a bag with vanilla ice cream, my other all-time favorite.
    "Oh, my goodness, you shouldn't have. Really, my thighs will not be happy. Let me get this ice cream into the freezer. Come on in," I said, grabbing Delaney's arm and leading him up the stairs into the living room.
    "Wow this is really nice, Taylor. Where's Morgan?" Delaney asked.
    "Thanks. Oh, Morgan's at home. I haven't even talked to her since she dropped me off the other morning," I responded.
    "My bad. I guess I assumed that you two were roommates," Delaney said with a puzzled look on his face.
    "No, I think the only roommates that I can have is of the nonhuman race. I live here with the members of the animal kingdom--my cat, Lacey, and my birds Gerald and Eddie," I responded.
    "Oh, really. I love cats. Where is yours?" Delaney asked as he looked around the living room.

"Wait here and make yourself comfortable. I'm going to put these flowers in the dining room and go let Lacey out of the room before she has a hissy fit. Can I get you anything?" I asked before heading upstairs.

"No, no I'm all right. Nothing right now," Delaney responded as he took a seat down on the huge white sofa in my living room.

When I came downstairs with Lacey in my arms, I found Delaney in the corner looking and talking to my birds.

"I see you've met Gerald and Eddie," I said as I stood beside Delaney with the overweight Lacey in my arms.

"Damn, that cat is huge. Come here, big girl," Delaney called to Lacey as he scooped her up.

"Why do you call your birds Gerald and Eddie?" Delaney asked.

"Because I love the whole Levert clan. I got my birds around the same time I started really listening to their music," I replied. I thought the names were fitting since they're so pudgy," I said.

"I guess from the names of your birds you listen to the *Tom Joyner Morning Show*. You know J. Anthony Brown and Tom Joyner are always making jokes about Eddie, Gerald and Sean Levert," Delaney stated.

"Yeah, I do. I can't go one day without listening to that show. I guess I do need to get new names for my birds since Eddie and Gerald have lost so much weight now," I responded.

Delaney found my photo album and began looking at my pictures. As I sat closely beside him, I could not help but take in the scent of his cologne.

"Delaney, what is that cologne you have on? It smells really good," I said, thinking that he not only smelled good, but sure did look good too.

"It's called Stylish Man. My boy sent it to me from Japan about three years ago. I haven't seen it here in the states yet. Every time I go out people ask me what the name of the cologne is," Delaney responded.

"Well it really smells good. So what movies did you bring?" I asked as I stood to head for the kitchen.

"I didn't know if you liked horror movies so I brought The Others and as backups I brought *Cooley High* and *Thirteen Ghosts*," Delaney said as he pulled the DVDs from the bag.

"Well, my favorite movie is *Cooley High*, so how about we watch that first. Can I get you some sweet potato pie?" I asked as I cut the pie and scooped the ice cream.

"Only if you'll have some with me," Delaney hollered from the living room.

I brought a tray with the ice cream and slices of pie into the living room and put the movie into the DVD player, and turned off the CD player.

"Why did you turn that off? I love Stevie Wonder," Delaney stated.

"Aren't you ready to watch the movie?" I asked.

"How about we eat this pie and ice cream, which I'm sure is going to be delicious. We can sit and talk for a few minutes. Those movies aren't going anywhere," Delaney suggested.

"That's cool. What do you want to know?" I asked as I reached for the bowl of ice cream.

"Well for one, I want to know why an attractive young woman like yourself is single and why hasn't anyone snatched you up?" Delaney asked.

"I don't know. I guess I never gave anyone the time to get to know me. I think because I lost my father at such a young age and my mother's second husband was such a negative influence, I've never trusted men after my father was gone. Therefore, I've never really given anyone the opportunity to get close to me," I explained.

"Taylor, I know that I just met you, but from what I can tell so far, you seem like you have a lot going for yourself. I told you that I am not about games and that I am truly anxious to get to know you. Now we can take things slowly if you'd like, but the way that I see it is tomorrow is not promised to anyone," Delaney stated.

"Well, I told you last night, I'm just as anxious to get to know you, but I would like to take things slowly. I think if we're going to contemplate the idea of being with each other then we really need to get to know each other's background. For instance, why aren't you seriously involved with someone yourself?" I asked.

"Like I told you before I've only been involved in two serious relationships. I was involved with one woman who had a lot of past issues relating to her son's father. The relationship was more of a hindrance than anything else. I don't have any children and I was not equipped to taking a backseat to someone else's child and the problems that go along with that whole scenario. When we would make plans to go out, there was always a situation that would arise that would preclude us from doing what we planned. After a while I just got fed up with the whole situation and decided to bail out," Delaney explained.

"This is a really personal question, but I need to know. Have you ever had an AIDS test?" I asked cautiously.

"I think that's probably the best question you've asked me so far. I'm not offended by your question. Yes, I've been tested several times. I'm HIV-negative. I haven't had sex in the last six months, so I haven't been tested recently. What about you?" Delaney questioned.

"I've also been tested, and I'm negative as well, but I've been celibate for two years," I responded.

I didn't want Delaney to get the wrong idea. I don't normally tell men this tidbit of information because they often want to "hit it" since it's like being with a virgin all over again. If and when I decide to resume having sex again, it's going to have to be for all the right reasons.

We continued to talk about ourselves and our upbringing and I learned that Delaney had some of the same problems with his father that I had with my mother. In fact, Delaney was the only boy. He had a sister who was two years younger. After what actually turned into five hours of talking and laughing, Delaney and I decided that since we both had to get up the next morning and go to work, that we would call it a night and we made plans for him to cook dinner for me that Wednesday night.

Lacey and I walked Delaney to the door.

"I hope you had a good time, Delaney, because I certainly did. I find that you are very easy to talk to. If nothing comes out of us getting to know each other, I hope that I have found a true friend in you. And I would like to thank you again for the flowers." I said, quickly glancing at the floor and blushing.

"Well, I hope that we can become more than friends, but for now, I will certainly accept that. Please do tell your mom that I really enjoyed the pie, and that she really put her foot in it. I look forward to meeting your mom and brothers soon. You all seem really close. In fact, your family's closeness reminds me of the relationship that I have with my mom and sister," Delaney stated.

What came next really surprised me. For the second time, Delaney grabbed my hand and kissed the back of it ever so gently.

"Taylor, I would really like nothing more than to kiss those soft, juicy lips, but I'm afraid that once I do, I won't want to stop. So I'll settle for a kiss on the back of your hand. That is unless you're feeling sorry for a brotha," Delaney said as he looked deeply into my eyes, that bright and cheerful smile making me want to devour him even more.

I moved a step toward Delaney and against my better judgment, kissed his lips gently. I took a step backward, but he placed his huge arm around my waist. I guess the look in my eyes told him that I wanted the kiss just as much, but that I had made a mistake.

"Taylor, I know that we're not ready for this. It's really too soon to kiss someone you hardly know, even though It seems as if I've known you for a long time. When I first saw you onstage and our eyes locked, I knew that you were someone I wanted to get to know. When you spoke those words, I felt your fire and I believe you sensed mine. When the time is right, things will be right. But for the record you have the softest, prettiest lips. And that's not just a line to be found in my poetry. Let me get out of here, before I get in trouble," Delaney stated as he turned to open the door.

"I'll see you on Wednesday. Should I bring anything?" I asked.

"Just bring that beautiful personality, your pretty smile, and your gorgeous self and I'll take care of the rest," Delaney responded as he headed for his SUV.

When I closed the door, I instantly ran upstairs to the bathroom. I pulled up my dress and took a peek at my thong underwear, to find that Delaney had indeed brought out feelings in me that I hadn't felt since I was in high school. I couldn't remember the last time when someone just stood close to me and brought this kind of reaction. Even when I spoke to him on the phone I got the same feeling. I guess that's what happens when you practice celibacy for two years. Somehow I didn't think my abstention was going to last too much longer. Not that I didn't want to do the right thing, but a girl has needs and based on how Delaney made me feel just standing near me, my hormones were beginning to awaken.

I took off my clothes, took another shower, got into the bed, and picked up the phone to call Morgan. As the phone continued to ring, I drifted off into a daydream about Delaney and me, wondering what it would be like to be with him intimately. I even fantasized about our wedding.

Let Morgan tell it, I live in a fairytale world. Realizing that Morgan was not in, I hung up, got on my knees, and prayed that the Lord would lead me into the right direction and safety for everyone dear to my life. After saying my prayers, I climbed into bed and drifted off into a sound sleep thinking of Delaney and how I really liked him, probably way too much, way too soon.

6/MORGAN

I heard the phone ringing, but I was in the shower and didn't feel like getting out to answer it. Let the machine pick it up. The way I figured, it could only be two people, Taylor or Mister. I didn't feel like talking, so I let myself relax under the hot water coming from the shower massager, a single girl's best friend.

Kofie had called me earlier in the evening while he was at work and we made plans to go to dinner and to a karaoke bar on Thursday. Since we both enjoyed Ms. Tootsie's, we decided to meet there for dinner and go singing afterward down on South Street. I'm no Anita Baker, but I do love to get my sing on.

I was expected in New York for a business trip, but I received a call early Sunday morning from my supervisor, informing me the meeting had to be postponed to the following week, due to a death in one of our client's family. Needless to say I was ecstatic about the change in plans. Don't get me wrong, I love to travel, it just gets to me from time to time.

On Monday, when I arrived to work at 7:00 A.M., I already had five messages on my voice mail. Normally Mondays and Fridays were hectic for me. I began working for Beckerman and Leechum Pharmaceuticals after graduating from Delaware State University. I am responsible for obtaining new business and new contracts for the company, and normally Mondays and Fridays are the days when our clients have decided if they will give us their company's business. I retrieved my messages from my voice mail, and when I heard Mister's voice on the phone I immediately deleted the message. Anything Mister wanted to say

Only Fools Gamble Twice

to me was useless at this point. I don't believe in mixing my personal life with business and I wasn't about to ruin my day with his nonsense. I tell you one thing, he was going stop leaving messages on my damn voice mail, or I was going to have to contact our legal unit. Enough was enough. He made his bed, now he would have to live with his decisions.

As I looked at my watch, I became angry because it was now 9:30 and my assistant, Rhonda, still hadn't bothered to show up for work yet. Rhonda was a woman about the same age as me. She was bright, fairly attractive, and a mother of two boys who were bad as hell. Whenever we had a family day at the job, those little punks would practically destroy the place. Rhonda always complained how it was so difficult to arrive to work on time and informed me each time she was late how I would know how hard it was one day--*when* and *if* I decided to ever settle down and have a family. I thought this was simply crazy. I know plenty of single parents who arrive to work on time and have to get their kids ready for school and day care. The sista is even married to a good husband who worked the night shift. Rhonda was just lazy, and that was that. I tried to calm myself down and thought that as of today Rhonda would be given a verbal warning, and then I'd recommend that she be fired altogether if she didn't get her act together. I didn't have time for the bullshit.

As I thumbed through the stack of work on my desk, my inside line rang, and I noticed from the Caller ID that it was my boss, Bernie.

"Good morning, Bernie. How are you doing this morning?" I asked cautiously.

Bernie, the only brother in a high-ranking position in the

Only Fools Gamble Twice

company, rarely called my line directly and when he did, he normally had either bad news or more work for me. I felt like neither this morning.

"Good morning, Morgan. Hope all is going well. I need to see you in my office. Stop by in a few minutes," he said blandly, not giving any indication as to what kind of mood he was in.

"I'll be right over," I responded, replacing the receiver. I grabbed my notebook and a cup of tea and headed over toward Bernie's office. I hated not knowing what I was walking into on a Monday morning. Something told me I wasn't going to like what he had to say. As I stepped out of my cubicle, I bumped into Rhonda, my notebook falling to the floor.

"Nice of you to show up, Rhonda," I said sarcastically as I bent to retrieve my notebook.

"Look, you don't understand, Morgan. I have two kids to get dressed and prepared for school. It's not always that easy to get here on time," Rhonda stated exasperated, all out of breath.

"Save it, Rhonda. I'm just about sick and tired of the excuses. Consider this your first verbal warning. If you're not here each morning by 8:30 like you were hired to be, then you will be terminated. Now do I make myself clear? I have a meeting with Bernie, so I need to cut this conversation short. I expect that work on your desk to be completed before you go to lunch," I stated sternly.

As I walked past Rhonda, I turned on my heel, adding "Oh yeah, I expect you to make up the time you missed this morning by working late this evening or taking personal time off," I added as I turned to walk away.

"Morgan, that's impossible. My husband has to go to

work early tonight. I don't know if I'll have anyone to pick up my kids from their after-school program and I don't have any personal time left. This is not fair!" Rhonda replied angrily, with her voice becoming louder.

I took a step closer and through clenched teeth, ensuring no one could hear our conversation, I added, "I'm late for my meeting. We'll discuss this later. For now, I suggest you make arrangements to stay late this evening," I replied as I turned my back and headed for Bernie's office.

I knew that Rhonda was still standing there watching me, so I decided to put a little bounce in my step. I thought, *If she knew what was good for her, she'd better get her ass back to work, or else.* The way my morning was beginning, first stupid-ass Mister leaving me messages, then this unexpected meeting with Bernie, and now this crap with pain-in-the-ass Rhonda working my nerves, I didn't know how much more stress I could take.

I approached Bernie's office and his secretary, Betty, was on the phone.

"Excuse me, would you please hold?" Betty politely said to the caller.

"Good morning, Morgan. Go right in. Mr. King is expecting you," Betty said in her butter-smooth voice.

"Thanks, Ms. Carpenter," I replied. Betty always insisted that I call her by her first name but I just couldn't bring myself to do that. As one of the few older African-American sisters in the company, I believe respect is due.

Betty Carpenter was probably the best-dressed woman in the company, extremely articulate, and always good natured. With her stylish gray hair, golden-brown complexion, and legs

Tina Turner would die for, she was definitely a lady who was probably considered a beauty queen in her day. In my opinion she was all of that.

    I casually walked into Bernie's office and he peered at me over his glasses. "Have a seat, Morgan." He gestured toward the huge leather chair in front of his large oak desk.

    "Morgan, you know I don't believe in beating around the bush, so I'll just come right out and say what's on my mind. Our company is planning a takeover of Remny Pharmaceuticals. This means even more business and more work for all of us here at Beckerman and Leechum. What I need from you is to extend your hours to include late nights and weekends until the takeover is official and a few weeks beyond that. I've spoken with the VP of Finance and he's approved my request for an increase in pay for you, an additional twenty percent bonus for night and weekend differential, so you can complete your assigned projects with adequate pay. I also need you to take on more responsibility on the floor. I need you to be the floor supervisor so I can pull the other section supervisors in to evaluate Remny's business operations. This will require everyone to pull an extra load. I selected you for this position because I know you're the right one for the job. Can I count on you, Morgan?" Bernie asked.

    I didn't know if I should be delighted or cry. I had been waiting patiently for a promotion like this for some time. I had heard rumors that our company was preparing a merger or takeover of another company, but I didn't know it would be this soon. The extra work wouldn't be too much of a problem since I didn't really have much of a social life anyway. I quickly convinced myself that this would be a great opportunity to show these folks just what I was made of and how us young black folks can really throw down with work when we needed to.

"Bernie, before I answer, I need to know if a few requests can be accommodated," I stated confidently.

"Let me know what you need and I'll see what I can do for you," Bernie responded with a hint of caution in his voice.

"Well for starters, I would like to work at home instead of putting in all of these hours, physically in the office on the weekends and nights, so I'd like a laptop computer. I would also like to know if I have the authority to hire and fire employees? And last but not least, I would like to have an office," I asked smoothly, not figuring this last request would be approved, but what the hell, a girl's gotta ask.

"I can get you a laptop with no problem. As far as the office goes, I think we should be able to handle that too. Get with Mike Jones about moving some desks closer together so we can make more space and have the technical unit set you up in Debbie Battle's former cubicle over the weekend. As far as the hiring and firing goes, I'd like you to run it pass me if you're planning on hiring or firing someone. Why? Do you have someone in mind?" Bernie asked.

"Yeah! Rhonda just doesn't seem to be working out. I'd like to keep some of our options open just in case we might want to let her go," I responded.

"Yeah, I know. Don't think I don't see what's going on out there. I am well aware of Rhonda's inability to get here on time. On that note, do what you have to do with her. I trust your judgment," Bernie stated.

With just five years on the job and all of thirty-five years

Only Fools Gamble Twice

old, Bernie was one of the youngest VPs at Beckerman and Leechum. He had recently married a white woman named Victoria who is the district manager in another department. They appeared to be a happy couple. Bernie could be weird at times, with his quiet demeanor, but he always treated me nicely and with respect and believed in standing up for his employees. Anytime I went to Bernie he always got things I needed to do my job more effectively. If he couldn't get them for me, he always explained why he couldn't get them or why I didn't need them.

Some of the sisters in the company had a problem with Bernie and Victoria's marriage, but who cares? If he can deal with it then who was I to object? It's not like I'd date him. It bothers me when black women get upset because black men date white women. I mean it's not like I've never dated a white guy. I used to go out with this white guy in high school. He was fine as all get out. After high school he went his way and I went mine. No harm, no foul. No big deal.

After Bernie and I discussed the work matters, we chatted about our weekends and our plans for the remainder of the summer. As it looked, I wasn't going to have much of a summer. I excused myself from the meeting. It seemed that I was going to be pretty busy. I explained to Bernie I had a lot of work cut out for me and I wanted to get started. I waved to Betty who was taking a phone call and she waved back.

When I reached my cubicle, I noticed Rhonda on the phone and overheard her talking about her personal issues with one of her friends. I thought how unprofessional she was and how I would go about relieving her of her duties within the next few weeks. As far as I was concerned, Rhonda was no longer needed at this company. With the new welfare-to-work initiative issues at the forefront of every political campaign, I would think every responsible adult would do everything in his power to demonstrate how good of an employee he was and ways to keep his job status. The way Rhonda was demonstrating her melancholy attitude, she would soon find out how hard it was to find and keep a good job. I took my seat and Rhonda immediately rolled her eyes and sucked her teeth.

"Girl, let me get off this phone and get this work done. I don't want to hear no crap from nobody about what I ain't doing around here. All right, girl. I'll talk with you later," Rhonda stated before she hung up the phone.

I figured I would give it a few minutes. I rang Rhonda's extension and told her I wanted to see her in the VPs' small conference room in fifteen minutes. Rhonda grunted about having to get all of her work completed, but I told her that this meeting pertained to her assignments and insisted that she meet me in fifteen minutes. I contacted the human resources department and asked if they could run a report for all qualified applicants who could possibly fill Rhonda's job. I asked that the file be mailed to me once completed. I checked my voice mail again and there were five priority calls about various accounts that I had been working on and one call from my mother. My mom didn't sound like her normal upbeat self, so I decided that I would call her back once I handled my business with Rhonda. I knew that my mother's birthday was coming up in July, which was a few weeks away, but I thought that maybe I should send her some flowers or a fruit basket to let her know how much she was appreciated.

My mother and I have always been very close. She and my dad tried to get me work in the field of law enforcement, like the state police or the CIA or something when I first graduated from DSU, but I wanted to do my own thing and law enforcement was not one of them. My mother had been losing some weight lately, not that she could afford to. She always stayed in the best possible shape, her being a former model and all. The weight loss was probably stress from the job, raising two children, and putting up with my father's crazy family. My dad's side of the family was enough to make anyone stressed. For now I had other pressing issues ahead of me.

I looked at my watch and noticed I had three minutes before my meeting with Rhonda. I pulled up the file I had been keeping on her time, attendance, and work performance and printed a copy for her and me. I always believe in getting the facts first so there is no room for unattractive arguments.

Just as I was getting up to head to the meeting, my phone rang and I hesitated before I answered. I figured I'd better at least take the call, not knowing if it was one of my accounts.

"Morgan Watson speaking," I blurted into the receiver.

"Well, look who's still alive. You don't have time for your friends over the weekend, huh?" Taylor responded.

"Hey, girl. I'm sorry I didn't call you back last night. I got in that shower and once I got out, that's all she wrote. A sista-girl was tired. Look, let me call you back in a few minutes. I have a quick meeting," I responded.

"Don't forget to call me. I have to tell you about my weekend with Delaney. Girlllll, I'm in love," Taylor said, sounding totally ridiculous.

"Stop trippin'. You just met the man. I'll call you back in few," I said, and I hung up the phone.

I knew that Taylor was just joking around, but still, she was moving way too fast.

I made my way to the conference room before Rhonda, knowing she would be late to that too. As I walked down the hall to the conference room, my feet sank in the comfort of the plush carpet. I entered the room and took my seat in the huge soft cushioned chair and reviewed the file again. Suddenly the door swung open and Rhonda sauntered in like she owned the place.

"All right. What is this all about? I have tons of work to complete and I don't have all day. But then again you already know that," Rhonda said rudely.

I was determined to handle this situation with all of the professionalism in my being. I took a few deep breaths and sat back in my chair.

"Please have a seat, Rhonda," I said, as I motioned at a nearby chair. "As discussed this morning, I explained that you are officially on verbal warning. I wanted to supply you with a copy of your performance folder to let you see on paper what your time, attendance, and work performance look like. Now if you'll notice there are quite a few mistakes that you've made on several integral accounts, not to mention your constant lateness and absences, all of which have been previously discussed with you," I stated calmly.

"Wait a minute. Hold up! What do you mean you were keeping a file on me? I might be your assistant, but you ain't my boss," Rhonda replied coldly.

"Well as a matter of fact, I was just asked by Mr. King to become the floor supervisor. So you are wrong in the statement you've just made. I am your supervisor as of a half hour ago. Now we can do this the hard way or the easy way. Once again, consider this your last warning. We're about to have some very important things transpire in this company and we all have to work much harder and much longer hours. If you don't think you can cut it then maybe you should find other means to support yourself and your family," I stated in my best professional tone.

"Yeah, I can make the cut," Rhonda replied, with a look of defeat on her face.

"That's great. I hope that we can take this situation and put it behind us. Let's move forward. We have a lot of work to get done so I think we need to get started ASAP. I have some files on my desk that need to be opened and completed," I responded with a smile, allowing Rhonda to save face.

Rhonda gave me half a smile. I knew she wasn't happy about me being her supervisor, but I guess her job was more important to her than I thought. She excused herself from the meeting and headed to her desk. Rhonda was also one of the few African-American women in the company and I began to feel sad that more people of color weren't reflected in the company. It seemed that some of us who do a good job every day go unrecognized. I just wished that I would be given an opportunity to be judged on my own merit, not by the standards of some lazy sista, who was messing things up for the next sista or brotha of color.

I gathered my belongings and headed back to my desk. I

returned my business calls, which took about two hours. Suddenly I noticed my stomach was growling. I began to order lunch from Sonny's, which was one of my favorite restaurants. I thought it might do me some good if I got out of the office for a while to get some fresh air. I called Sonny's to order my usual, which consisted of sliced roasted turkey breast over a huge bowl of mixed salad greens, with low-fat Thousand Island dressing. I knew by the time I arrived, Sonny the owner, would have my order ready to go and it would taste exactly the way I loved it.

    Before forwarding my phone to the operator, I informed Rhonda that I would be stepping out for lunch and would return shortly. I asked if she wanted anything and she told me no and continued to work diligently at her desk. I smiled inwardly. At least our conversation was working. All she really needed was a good warning to get on the right track.

    I stepped outside and was instantly happy that I'd decided to get some fresh air. It was pretty hot, especially for a June day, but I didn't mind because the hot weather felt like a comfortable blanket that left me feeling warm all over.

    I crossed Rodney Square at the light and turned on Fifth Street and instantly saw Mister. I was so wrapped up my thoughts that I hadn't even thought that I might just see him outside. Mister worked just two blocks from my office at a large downtown finance company. Before I could turn and walk the other way, he spotted me so I continued my stride and looked straight ahead. Just as I thought he would allow me to pass without saying anything, he ran between cars and crossed the street, quickly catching up to me.

    "I know you're headed Sonny's. I bet I know what

Only Fools Gamble Twice

you ordered for lunch too. You are so predictable, Morgie. We were meant to be together," Mister said, flashing his even white teeth.

If I had an ounce of sense I would have slapped the cow dung out of that fool. Who the hell did he think he was to keep playing with my emotions like that? I know that everyone thinks I'm this strong and powerful person, but a woman can only take so much.

Mister was right in some aspects. He knew me too well, sometimes better than I knew myself. Although I knew this, I would never tell him so.

"What is it? What do you want?" I asked, feeling powerless. I just didn't have the strength to argue with this butt head another minute.

"I just want to walk with you. I'm on my way to Sonny's too," he said, but we both knew he was lying.

"You think you know me so well. For your information I'm not going there. I'm going to that little deli up on Walnut Street," I said.

"See now I know you're lying. You know that you're going to Sonny's. You've never even been inside of that deli. Just to prove how much I know you, I'll just walk with you," Mister stated smoothly.

"That won't be necessary. I'm a big girl and I am quite capable to taking care of myself. You probably don't remember, but I've been doing exactly that since you found that you need your space," I replied sarcastically.

"Here we go. I guess you just can't let shit go. Come on get it out. I knew that was coming. I guess I walked right into that one," Mister stated with frustration.

I had to literally bite down hard on my tongue. If it's one thing I'm known for it's my opinion, and I was definitely about to rip Mister a new asshole. I had so many things to say to him, and it was most surely going to be said, at one time or another, but in the middle of downtown Wilmington was not the place.

I kept walking and thought that if I moved faster he would get the message, but he didn't. When we approached the deli I kept walking and out of the corner of my eye I could see him beaming as he realized that he had caught me in a lie. I rolled my eyes and turned the corner and crossed the street to Sonny's.

"All right, you've had your little laugh and you were right, so you can go now," I said as I turned to head into Sonny's.

Mister jumped ahead of me to grab the door handle, trying to act as if he were a gentleman. Please, I knew the bastard when.

"I know, but I haven't eaten yet, so I think I'll just grab something to eat while I'm here," Mister said as he held the door open for me. When Mister and I entered Sonny's restaurant, Sonny had a surprised look on his face.

"What? What in the world. Never mind. Don't answer. Let me mind my own business. You young folks have a way of changing your mind like you change underwear," Sonny said as he threw up his hands.

"It ain't that kind of party," I replied to Sonny.

"Sweetie, like I said, don't answer. Your food is ready. You want to eat here or take it out?" Sonny asked. Before I could reply, Mister answered for me.

"She'll eat it here. Let me have a turkey and cheese sandwich and a beer on tap too, boss man, while you unwrap her food." Mister stated, as I looked at him with a dumbfounded look.

"Excuse me, but I don't have the time or desire to eat lunch here. Especially not with you," I said matter-of-factly.

"Now come on, girl. You don't have time to eat with an old friend?" Mister asked, flashing that damn smile in my face. "C'mon, my treat. As long as you don't try to take advantage of me, lunch is on me," Mister stated as he motioned for me to a seat in the rear of the restaurant.

"Fine, but I only have about twenty-five minutes to spare and then I have to get back to work. Some of us have real jobs, you know," I replied as Mister tried to placed his hand on my waist, then removed it when I gave him a look of disgust.

Mister stepped back and motioned me with his hand, allowing me to walk in front of him as he directed me toward what used to be our table. There he was again trying to be Mr. Gentleman of the Damn Year. Well that crap wasn't working here, not today.

Sonny's was a place where Mister and I frequently met for lunch while we were a hot item. It wasn't that crowded because most people opted to have their food delivered or simply came into the restaurant to pick it up.

Sonny was special to me because he was one of my dad's fraternity brothers. Wednesday through Friday nights, most of the young professionals in downtown Wilmington would gather for drinks and hot wings after work. Sonny's was notorious for its spicy hot wings, collard greens, and corn bread. He had known that Mister and I had broken up, but being a good friend of my father's and not wanting to get involved with young folks' business, Sonny had always stayed neutral. One time he did caution me to keep an eye on that "young fool," as he casually referred to Mister. Sonny believed that Mister had yet to experience the art of knowing when you had a good woman and how to treat her right, with respect and honor.

When we arrived at the table, Mister jumped in front of me and pulled out my chair. After we were seated, he immediately began to speak nonstop, which was rather unusual for him. The whole time we lived together, I could barely get him to complete an entire sentence. I read somewhere that women use something like 100,000 words a day and men use about half of that. When women get home they go into second gear, while men have used all of their words for the entire day at work. That's the reason why men don't really communicate once they're home and women can't seem to understand the whole thing. Totally frustrating to me. I guess I need to find my next man at work. At least then I'll get to hear him talk while we're there.

"Morgan, I'm sorry about those messages I left you. I was angry with you for not returning my phone calls. But the truth of the matter is that was all bullshit. I know that I hurt you and it may sound like a cliché, but I never meant to hurt you," Mister stated.

"But you did hurt me. I don't know what you expect from me. I don't have a clue why you still call me. On the one hand, you act like I despise you, then on the other hand you blow up my pager, cell phone, and answering machine like I'm the last woman on Earth. How am I suppose to deal with all of this shit?" I exploded, no longer able to hold my feelings inside.

"I wish I could take back the pain I caused you. I just don't know what to say. Can't we just be friends for now? See where this whole thing leaves us? Maybe we're meant to be together. I don't know. I just needed some time to sort out my feelings," Mister responded as he looked directly into my eyes.

I felt uneasy with Mister looking so intently at me. I knew that if I returned the gaze I could be sucked back into his heart and his lies all over again. I wondered how he could appear so happy and content about our relationship one day and then just throw it all away with not so much as a care in the world. How could we be friends when I still had strong feelings for him?

Perhaps he thought he knew how he felt about me, but I knew exactly how I felt about him. There hasn't been a day that's gone by that I haven't thought about picking up the phone probably a million and one times to call him. In order for me to get him out of my system I had to do this cold turkey. No calls to him and none from him. After today, this would be the last time he and I would share company. It had to be this way. I knew that he still cared for me and all, but I had to preserve my feelings. I couldn't take the chance that he would hurt me so intently again. I was just going to have to do what I had to do. There were too many miles on my index finger already from the times I'd called this bastard.

Just then Sonny approached the table with our food. I thanked him and he asked if we needed anything else. Mister told him we didn't and Sonny left to return to the bar. I began eating my salad and as usual, it was delicious. At this point I really didn't want to hear anything Mister had to say about our past relationship or some fake future friendship. I just wanted to eat my salad in peace. Mister must have sensed my mood because he changed the subject and started telling me about his brother, his sister-in-law, and their overactive daughter. I told Mister about my promotion and he appeared to be genuinely happy for me. After I ate, I continued to explain how Rhonda was getting on my nerves and how the promotion had brought me more responsibility. Mister and I continued to chat and I realized I stayed out much longer than I wanted. Mister paid the bill, left a generous tip for Sonny and we made our way out of the restaurant. I gave Sonny, a wave and he nodded as he continued to fuss around the restaurant.

We arrived back at Mister's building first. He kissed me lightly on the cheek and asked if he could meet me Friday, after work at Sonny's.

"I'm going to be working late on Friday. I won't be able to go," I replied.

Don't ask me why I just didn't tell Mister that I would not be talking to him for some time to come, but I just didn't want it to go down like that. I figured if he thought things were on the up and up he wouldn't pursue me as heavily. I'd just leave things like that.

"Maybe you can stop by after you get off work. I know everyone will still be there."

"I don't think so. I have so much to do this weekend," I responded.

"Alright. Hopefully I'll see you on Friday, baby," Mister replied, ignoring my evasiveness. Mister turned on his heel. He then kissed me again on my cheek. He didn't say anything, he just turned around as I watched him walk away. I didn't say anything either. I was sad because I had lost a great friend and a damn good lover, but I needed to look out for me. If I didn't, who would?

    I slowly began to head back to work. I thought about all the games men play and I was just sick of it. I know that I wanted to be married with children someday and yet I got so frustrated because I was so far removed from that lifestyle, with no immediate end in sight. I needed a man who knew what he wanted and was happy to share a meaningful life with me. I didn't care if I lived to be a hundred years old I'd never understand how men could go from loving you one day to acting as if they didn't even know you the next day.

    When I arrived back to work, I had seven messages from clients and one special message and a bouquet of yellow roses. When I opened the card, I couldn't help but smile. The roses were from Kofie. The card read:

I'm so glad that I met you, I look forward to our date on Thursday evening. Call me on my cell phone, 267- 555-5223. Thinking of you.

-K-.

    I couldn't remember if I had given Kofie my work number, then it dawned on me that I hadn't. I immediately called the number Kofie had provided and he answered on the second ring.

    "Kofie speaking," his strong accent came through the phone.

    "Hi Kofie, this is Morgan," I replied.

"Hello, Morgan. I see you received the roses. I hope you like them," he said.

"They're lovely. Thanks so much. Listen, how did you get my business number?" I questioned. I know I can sometimes be a bit paranoid, but I needed to know.

"I hope you don't mind. I had Delaney contact Taylor and she called the florist for me with your business address. She didn't give me the information. I just wanted to show my appreciation for our conversation and to hopefully put a smile on your beautiful face," Kofie responded.

I now became a bit more relaxed. I was glad Taylor didn't give him my personal information. That's all I needed was another stalker on my hands. It was bad enough Mister harassed me every chance he got.

"It was very kind of you. I don't mind at all," I said with a smile.

"I also look forward to our date on Thursday. How about I call you tomorrow night and we can arrange all the details?" he stated.

"If you could call me Wednesday that would be better. Tomorrow I'll be tied up," I replied.

"Great, than I'll call you Wednesday. Have a good day and stay sweet," Kofie flirted before we said our good-byes.

I had to admit that I surely loved his accent. The flowers were a nice touch too. Slowly, I was beginning to get out of my slump. Thursday, we would have a great time and I was starting to get excited by it all. For the moment, I had tons of work and calls to return.

7/TAYLOR

Wednesday proved to be as hectic as I imagined it would be for me at work. My team leader, Charlotte, who is miserable as all hell, constantly finds something to complain about, any chance she gets.

I had spoken to Delaney earlier in the day while he was also at work. We confirmed our dinner plans for later that evening at his house in Greenville. I'm not really familiar with that area, so I got directions from Delaney, which seemed quite confusing.

Before I left work, I got in a quick workout and a nice hot shower. So what if it was eighty-nine degrees outside? The hotter the water the better it was for me to relieve stress. I had a gift certificate to a local black-owned spa, Defying Styles, in New Castle, and as soon as I found the time, I was heading straight for my massage. A sista was tense. Like I said, my supervisor was driving me up a wall. After my shower, I quickly changed from my work attire into a red, mid-length silk sundress, pulled my hair on top of my head, and was out of the office and on the road by 6:15 P.M.

I stopped at the liquor store and purchased a bottle of White Zinfandel since I remembered Delaney said that he liked it as well. I arrived at his home at 6:35.

When I pulled up to Delaney's home I was truly impressed. The brother's crib had it going on. He lived in a huge, three-story, old historic single-family home in the heart of where the well-to-do live. Nice, very nice. I had to admit that my cheap bottle of Zinfandel was making me feel very out of place. Then I had to shake it off. Delaney didn't come off like some snob who wore his Jack'n Jill card on his sleeve. He was obviously a down-to-earth kind of guy, despite his current financial portfolio.

When I rang the doorbell, Delaney answered, looking very sexy as usual in a pair of beige linen trousers, white tank top and a pair of leather sandals. Very nice, or as the Spanish say, *muy bien.*

"Hey, sweetness," Delaney said as he greeted me with a hug.

"Whew! Or should I say Damn!" I said as I accepted his warm embrace.

"What's that all about? Come on in and get out of this heat."

"Oh, I love the heat, it doesn't bother me at all. When you're a winter baby like me and grew up in that cold weather, you definitely welcome the heat any chance you can get," I explained and extended the bottle of wine to Delaney.

"Are you trying to get me drunk so you can have your way with me?" Delaney asked with a raised eyebrow.

"Only if you want me to," I said, not believing that I had just let those words come out of my mouth.

"Whew. You sure you didn't have a glass or two before you came over?" Delaney teased.

"Let me stop. I can't believe I said that," I said, now becoming embarrassed.

"Freudian slip, huh?" Delaney questioned.

"You know it. Freud wasn't right about a lot of things, but he got me on that one," I stated. "What's for dinner?" I questioned, trying to change the very heated subject.

"Veal chops, new potatoes, and string beans. I remembered that you don't eat pork. Hope you like them. I got off around noon today. I finished one of the programs I've been working on for the past few weeks and I'm looking forward to taking some much-deserved time off for a mini vacation. I'm going to go see my family in Arkansas next week," Delaney explained.

Delaney and his family were originally from West Helena, Arkansas. His mother and father packed their kids up when Delaney was around two and moved to Philly. Soon afterward, his parents divorced, but his mom relocated to Arkansas a few years ago. His mom was looking forward to having a little family reunion to get them all together before the summer was over, he explained.

"Yeah, that should be really nice. I'd love to get away this summer, but I don't think it's going to happen. Besides, Morgan and I are supposed to be going to the Bahamas in September. I guess I can wait until then to get my rest on," I explained.

"Oh, I know you two are going to be off the chain on that getaway. Two young, pretty ladies off on some deserted island. Now you know you two are going to have all of the men going buck wild," Delaney teased.

"No, we've been once before. We went to a few of the clubs on the island, but we've pretty much had our share of wild and crazy days. For the most part it's just R&R," I explained.

Morgan and I had gone to the Grand Bahamas last year when she and Mister were going through problems. Quite naturally, two single, attractive women on an island filled with a bunch of men only too eager to make our acquaintance was what we experienced. We were far from trying to be mesmerized by the whole situation. If you think about it, those men see hundreds of thousands of women every year, so you're just another pretty face. I can't get with that whole Stella stuff. If I want to get my groove back or on, I can do it in the states. I don't need some male gigolo named Dexter trying to sow his oats on or in me.

"Yeah, I can understand that. You know I'm going to miss you when I go," Delaney said, looking ever so seductive in those linen trousers.

"Miss me? Why would you do that? You just met me," I said sincerely.

"Because I like you. Is that too hard to understand?" Delaney asked, as he stepped forward and kissed the tip of my nose.

"Not at all. I'm going to miss you too," I confessed. "So when are you leaving?" I wished I could go with him, but I knew it was way too soon to meet his family and go on a vacation with a guy I just met over the weekend.

"Probably in a few weeks or so. We're all still trying to coordinate our schedules. But I'll let you know as soon as I know. What about going down to the shore with me this next weekend to spend some time together before I head off? Don't answer yet. Think about it first. C'mon, let's eat. I'm starving," Delaney said, leading me to the dining room.

What? Go away with him? How could he say something like that, but expect me not to have a reaction. The idea sounded great, but I knew there was no way I could go. What would I wear? Where would I sleep? I needed to get a Brazilian

Only Fools Gamble Twice

wax, my nails done, so many things to do. Wait a minute. I couldn't even begin to contemplate this. Or could I? You only live once, right? No, there's no way I could go. I hardly knew this man.

The way Delaney's house was situated, the dining room had to be entered into from a set of double doors. When he opened the doors, I was completely amazed. The room was surrounded by candlelight and the food was already on the plates. Although I had brought a bottle of wine, there was wine in the glasses. There was no light except the illumination from the candles. There was also a dozen of yellow and red roses on the credenza.

"For you," Delaney said, handing me the roses.

"Thanks, Delaney. They're beautiful," were the only words I could immediately say.

After Delaney pulled out my chair, he hurried over to the wall unit to hit the power button on the stereo system, turning on our favorite song, "Ribbon in the Sky." At that moment, all of the day's troubles vanished as I sat back, took a sip of my wine, and realized who I was falling for this guy named Delaney who sat before me. I also realized that there was no way in the world that I wasn't going to the shore the following weekend with him. Absolutely no doubt in my mind. You only live once and I wouldn't be young forever. I've got to do what I've got to do. To be on the safe side, I was going to see if we could invite Morgan and Kofie, you know to keep it all good.

During dinner Delaney and I talked about everything-- our families and our college days. Not only was Delaney a great host, but the meal he prepared was absolutely fantastic.

Apparently, Delaney's mother worked two jobs after his parents divorced, so early on he learned to cook for himself and his younger sister.

"Dinner was great. I really enjoyed myself. Now it's my turn to show off my cooking skills to you," I said.

"Just let me know when and where," Delaney responded.

"Do you think you'll still be able to come over this weekend for the fight party?" I asked.

"Sure, I just need to get a few things in order for my trip, then I'm all yours," Delaney responded.

"All mine, huh?" I flirted. What was wrong with me? This man was bringing out the beast in me. I knew what it was. Those two years of celibacy were finally catching up with me.

"If you want it, you got it," Delaney said as he spread his arms, offering God knows what.

I had to side-step that one. Goodness knows where that could have ended.

"I'll throw a little something-something together this weekend for the fight party and show off my skills," I stated.

"Do you need me to make something? I make a great strawberry shortcake," Delaney offered.

"No, I love strawberries, but hate strawberry shortcake," I responded.

"Really? So you like strawberries, huh? What about whipped cream," Delaney asked seductively, taking us immediately back to where I just steered us away.

"Yeah, it's weird. I like strawberries and I like whipped cream, and of course I love cake, it's just that I don't like strawberry shortcake," I responded, not feeding into Delaney's flirtation.

"Well just let me know what you want me to bring to your party. I can practically make any kind of dessert. Or if you want me to bring some kind of seafood salad or something just let me know," Delaney offered, now getting back on track.

"Just make sure you're there, that's all I care about," I stated.

"Why is it so important that I'm there?" Delaney asked.

"You know, you ask too many questions," I responded.

"Me? You're always the one who wants to know why I like you or something," Delaney said.

"Because I like you that's why," I responded as I stepped closer and kissed Delaney on the nose like he had done to me earlier.

"Oh, so you like me, huh?" Delaney asked, grabbing me around my waist.

"Yeah, I do," I said, placing my arms around his waist.

"And why is that?" Delaney asked.

"What did I tell you about all of those questions?" I asked.

Delaney pulled me tighter, his rock-hard body pressed against mine. He planted a kiss ever so gently on my lips. I allowed the tension of the week to be released and my body became limp in his arms. I had to admit I was forgetting who and where I was for a moment when Delaney abruptly stopped kissing me. He then led me to the living room and we both sat on the sofa, music playing softly throughout his home. The lights were down low and the whole atmosphere was simply perfect. Delaney turned me around so my back was to his chest. He then began to gently massage my temples, then my shoulders, my arms, and finally my fingers. I was totally relaxed and then he planted a wet, sensuous kiss on the back of my neck.

"Would you like some dessert? I have some ice cream in the freezer," Delaney whispered.

"No. I'm just fine," The dessert that I wanted wasn't in the freezer. *Stop it!* I had to tell myself.

"Don't stop. That feels good," I whispered.

"You like that?" Delaney asked, through wet kisses on the back of my neck. He blew softly into my ear between gentle kisses.

"Please don't do that," I pleaded, trying to turn around to face Delaney.

"No, I want you to stay right there. You had a hectic week, and I want you to totally relax. Now I know that you enjoy kisses, so just allow me to make you feel good. Is that too much to ask?" Delaney whispered softly in my ear.

"It's just that you happen to be kissing me in very sensitive spots. It's making me light-headed," I whispered.

"Woman, just go with the flow," Delaney whispered again in my ear. He continued to place even more sensuous kisses on my neck and ear.

After what seemed like several thousand more kisses and when I could no longer take it anymore, I had to think of a way to stop this situation from escalating. I thought I was going to have an orgasm right there on the man's sofa. I couldn't think of the last time I felt so good. Yes I could, two years ago. Even then, it didn't feel like this. As a matter of fact, I couldn't ever remember feeling this damn good.

"I need to use the ladies' room," I said.

"Upstairs, third door on your right," Delaney replied.

When I reached the bathroom, I checked the linen closet for a washcloth. I washed my face and had to take the opportunity to freshen up a bit. It had been ten years since graduating from high school, but I felt like a teenager, like this was the first time I had been kissed by a guy. I couldn't believe the physical reaction that was coming from my body each time Delaney planted one of those kisses on me. I placed the washcloth in the hamper and returned downstairs.

When I returned to the living room, Delaney had his eyes closed and his head leaning on the back of the couch.

"I hope you don't mind, but I used one of the washcloths in the linen closet," I said.

"No, no problem. Is everything okay?" Delaney asked with concern.

"Yes, yes, everything is fine. It's just that I needed to cool off a bit. You don't mind if I sit over here in this chair, do you?" I asked, trying to calm my hormones down a bit.

"Now, why are you doing a thing like that to me? I know I smell good, I even took a bath before you came over," Delaney said, lifting his underarm to smell himself.

"Oh no. That's just the problem. You smell a little too good for me. You're driving me crazy. I just need some time to calm down," I replied as I fanned myself.

"Oh, really?" Delaney said as he stood and walked over to my chair.

"What are you doing?" I asked. I couldn't stand this man being so close without feeling excitement all over. His body's chemistry was driving me wild. Delaney reached beyond me and grabbed a book from the shelf behind the chair.

"I have a poem I wrote that I want you to read to me," Delaney said as he squeezed in the chair, sitting so close that I could feel his breath on my neck. He flipped open the book and turned to the poem he wanted me to read.

"Hold on. Before you do, I need a refill on my wine. Can I get you another glass?" Delaney asked as he headed for the kitchen.

"No thanks. I have to drive and, besides, I think I had one too many," I said.

"But you only had one glass. You had more than that the other night," Delaney hollered from the kitchen.

"Yeah, but I wasn't here alone with you, relaxing and feeling the way that I do now the other night either," I responded.

"So tell me exactly how is it that you feel?" Delaney said, shutting off the kitchen light and coming back to the living room.

"I think we both know how I feel," I said as Delaney peered at me with those dark eyes as he sipped his wine.

"I want you to tell me," Delaney replied.

"You make me feel good, okay," I said, slightly embarrassed.

"Was that so hard? To make you feel better, I'll let you know you make me feel fantastic! Okay, now I said it and it's out there," Delaney responded.

"How is it that I make you feel that good and you were the one doing all of the kissing and what-not?" I asked.

"You don't have to touch me to make me feel good. Just seeing you enjoying the moment and relaxing makes me feel good. Besides, I like the way you enjoy me touching you. The

Only Fools Gamble Twice

way you try to fight it instead of going with your feelings," Delaney responded.

"I'm afraid to trust my feelings. It's been so long since I've felt that good. I don't trust my own judgment," I said, allowing my true feelings to be revealed. Delaney was easy to talk to and I didn't want to start off our new relationship by playing games.

"Taylor, we've already agreed to take things slowly. I'm not going to do anything that would jeopardize your trust for me and you and me getting to really know each other. We're both adults and if and when that time comes to get closer that'll happen. For now, let's enjoy the romantic feelings and passion that only new relationships experience. I want both of us to feel good, but at the same time I don't want to rush things either. I know how to impose self-restraint," Delaney said.

"Well I do as well, it's just that I definitely want to take things slowly. I don't want to make any foolish decisions," I responded.

"Me either. Now enough talking. Are you going to read my poem to me or not?" Delaney asked, squeezing back into the chair beside me. His rock-hard legs felt so good against mine. For now, I had to concentrate.

> *Friendship is both true and dear,*
> *its bond grows stronger from year to year*
> *It's built with trust, understanding, and love.*
> *It's kept with honesty and prayers to God above.*
> *It's sharing the good times along with the bad.*
> *It's showing your emotions whether glad, mad, or sad.*
> *It's taking time out of a busy day to throw a quick smile*
> *of encouragement your way.*

It's being there to show you care through snow, sleet, or rain,

I pray this friendship I share with you will always remain.

"That was really pretty. When did you write that?" I asked.

"The night I met you," Delaney said.

"Oh, really? It's great to know that I'm such an inspiration," I replied.

"Yeah, I've been having writer's block for some time now and when I met you the other night, I came home and wrote it from the top of my head. See what you do to me?" Delaney said.

"We should go to another spot for poetry night. I hear Savannah's and Gloria's Soul Food Café have poetry nights too. Maybe you can read it at one of those spots for me some time," I said.

"For you? Anything," Delaney replied.

It was getting late and I had to find my way out of Greenville. I also knew that my mother would be calling soon, wondering where I was. I offered to help Delaney clean the kitchen and after a few minutes of bickering, he finally gave in. After the kitchen and dining room were spotless, Delaney and I shared a few more kisses in the kitchen and things started to slowly get heated. As we stood in front of the sink, I felt Delaney's hardness pressed against my leg. I started gyrating my hips. You know like everyone used to do in high school. Thoughts of making passionate love to Delaney crossed my mind several hundred times. Delaney pulled one of my legs around his waist and picked me up, placing me on the kitchen sink.

He planted wet, passionate kisses on my forehead, eyes,

nose, and neck. I let out a low sigh. This situation was now completely out of hand. I could no longer stand these bottled-up celibate feelings of mine.

"I think it's time for me to leave now," I whispered.

"Yeah, I think you'd better go home now," Delaney whispered in return.

Delaney lifted me from the kitchen sink and we held hands as we walked through the dining room. I gathered my purse and my roses and headed for the front door. At the front door there was a repeat performance of kissing and grunting and then I had to force myself to leave. I gave Delaney one last kiss on the lips and then I turned his head and whispered into his ear.

"I had a wonderful time. Thanks for the roses, and I'm missing you already," I said as I followed my statement with a gentle kiss on Delaney's ear.

Delaney grabbed both of my hands tightly. "Please! Don't do that," he said through gritted teeth.

"Oh, I'm sorry. You don't like that?" I asked, concerned.

"No. It's a very weak spot for me," Delaney said, his teeth still gritted.

"Oh, you can dish it out, but can't take it, huh?" I asked, laughing at his expression.

"Oh, I can take it. It's just that I wasn't expecting that," Delaney responded.

"So you mean to tell me that if I did it again, that you could take it this time?" I asked.

"Most definitely," he responded.

"Okay. Here it comes," I said as I turned his face toward my mouth. "Delaney, I like the way this makes you feel," I said, as I kissed and blew softly in Delaney's ear.

"Okay. You win. Stop it!" Delaney said. As he adjusted himself, I couldn't help but laugh. The sight of seeing two grown people who obviously were attracted to each other holding off from pleasing each other until the time was appropriate was humorous to me. At that moment, I wanted to give myself completely to Delaney, but my moral upbringing kept telling me it was way too soon. My body on the other hand was screaming to be pleased.

"Okay. I'd better get going before I snatch you up," I stated.

"Than why don't you stay?" Delaney teased.

"I think we both know the answer to that question. Really, I've gotta get going. See you, sweetie," I said. I gave Delaney one last kiss on the cheek.

"Drive safely and call me when you get home," Delaney said.

On the drive home, I decided to call Morgan. When I turned on my cell phone I realized I had a voice mail message. It was from Mr. Boxer Man, Bruce. I called him back and he actually picked up the phone.

"Hello," he drooled into the phone.

"Hi, Bruce. This is Taylor. I got your message. How are things going?" I asked.

"What things?" he asked.

"Nothing particular, you know, I'm just asking what's been going on?"

"Oh, nothing. I'm just training hard for my next fight," he explained. I couldn't quite put my finger on it, but something wasn't right with this dude. "So when can I take you out, pretty?" he asked.

"Oh, I don't know," I said, searching for a reason why I didn't quite feel ready to go out with this guy.

"I been trainin' and workin' hard and I need a sexy lady on my arm so I can sport around town," he said.

"Really now? By the way, where do you work?" I asked.

"I work at the Burger Castle. Let me know if you ever come through the drive-through and I can hook you up. I usually work on fries, but I'm in the runnin' for a promo to the grill. I just work there to make a little money on the side while I do my training. I'm the next middleweight champion of the world you know," he explained.

"Oh, okay. If I ever stop through, I'll ask for you," I responded.

"How many kids you got?" he asked.

"I don't have any children. And you?" I asked.

"You ain't got no kids? Man, That's wassup. I got five," he boasted proudly, as if he were going to make me his next baby's mother.

"Five?" I slowly repeated.

"So when you gon' let me take you out? My ride ain't up and runnin' right now, but I see you got a phat whip so you can just pick me up, right?"

Now, don't get me wrong, but this is where I exit stage right or left, but at any rate I'm exiting right now. The writing is on the wall. This butt head is just plain stupid.

"Let me call you back. I'll call you when I get in the house," I lied. *Forgive me, Father.*

"What time you gon' be in the house," he asked before I could press the end button.

"I should be there by no later than quarter after nine. Call me back on my cell phone then," I said, knowing full well I would probably have to change my jogging route and block his number from my cell phone.

"Quarter after. What time you gon' call me?" he asked again.

"Quarter after should be good. Call me then," I repeated.

"Quarter after? What dat mean?" he asked.

"What do you mean? What does that mean? Quarter after nine," I repeated.

"I mean what time is that on the clock. Is that when the little hand is on the…" he began.

The sound *click* was the last thing he heard. There was no way I was going to explain to some grown-ass man how to tell time. I couldn't believe that crap.

After that, I couldn't quite concentrate. I just drove with my mouth hanging open, in utter shock.

When I arrived home, I noticed I had three messages. One from my mom, one from Delaney, and the third from my brother Tyrone.

For my brother to call me was pretty strange. I first dialed Delaney's number.

"Hey, sweetness," he said into the receiver.

"How did you know it was me?" I asked, a bright smile spreading across my face.

"Ah, a little gadget called Caller ID," he said

sarcastically.

"Ha, ha. Very funny," I replied.

"What are you about to do? Go to bed?"

"No, I have to make a few phone calls then I'm off to get my beauty rest."

"Before you go to bed, I want you to call me. I can't stop thinking about you."

"Oh, really. Tell me more," I responded.

"Call me back and I'll make sure you hear it all," he said, sounding sexier by the minute.

"Most definitely," I responded in a low, sexy voice.

After hanging up the phone, I pressed the speed dial button for my mom's number and the phone rang about ten times, before it was answered by a man whose voice unfamiliar.

"Yeah?" the irritated voice yelled into the receiver.

"Who's this?" I carefully asked.

"Who do you want to speak to?" the voice responded angrily.

"I want to speak to my mother. Who's this?" I said, now becoming equally as angry.

"Taylor, you're going to have to call her back. I'm on the line long distance," the angry, yet distantly familiar voice responded. Before I could respond, the person disconnected the call and I was left holding the receiver, getting a dial tone in my ear. I racked my brain to figure out who it could be and then in dawned on me that it was the bastard from hell. My younger brother's father, Winston.

Winston was the asshole who had brought my mother down after my dad died and the person who had gotten her strung out on drugs. What was he doing there, answering my mother's phone? It was all beyond me. That explained why Tyrone had called and left me a message. He was probably calling to warn me. Let's just say Winston and I despised each other.

I dialed the number again and this time my mother answered the phone. "Mom? What the heck is going on? Why on earth would Winston be answering your phone?"

"First of all, who do you think you're talking to? Taylor, don't start your nonsense. This is my house and what I decide to do in it is my business."

"What do you mean it's your business? Have you forgotten how he had you strung out on drugs and practically ruined your life, not to mention what he did to the rest of this family?" I yelled into the receiver.

"Taylor, that was a long time ago. Winston is clean now. He's a little down and out right now and I'm not going to turn my child's father away like that. He'll be staying with us for a while. This *is* still my house," Mom stated.

"I don't believe this. I can't believe you're going to just let him walk back in your life like that. After all we've done to get this family back on track, here he comes and tries to destroy us. I can't believe you're just going to allow Satan to dwell in your home."

"Taylor, stop. Everyone deserves a second chance."

"I'll talk to you later, Mom," I said before I hung up the phone.

I just couldn't believe what I was hearing. I sat on my bed and must have cried for about an hour. All my mom's hard work to get her life back on track was going down the drain. All the worrying she did about me and my life and who I went out with and everything, and now she was letting this evil spirit back into her life and her home. I didn't know what to do other than pray. I prayed like I never had before. I prayed for my mother's deliverance and for Winston to be removed from her house. It was on now. This demon in her house had to go!

I awakened Saturday morning sore and disoriented. My arm was swollen and it felt like a freight train had run across my back.

I hadn't spoken to Delaney since Wednesday night and I knew that he was beginning to worry. He had already left several messages for me and I just wasn't up to talking to him just yet. On top of that, I had lucked up and gotten Morgan's answering machine so I could call her and cancel the fight party. I just didn't feel like being bothered by anyone. This week had surely turned into a true nightmare.

On Thursday, when I arrived at work, Tyrone called me around ten and was frantic.

"Tay, this Ty. Why didn't you call me back last night?"

"I called and Winston answered then I called Mom and…" "I ain't living there no more," Ty blurted.

"What? What do you mean? What the hell happened?"

"Winston tried to step to me and I told him I wasn't having that shit."

"Watch your mouth," I said.

"Aw, my bad. Anyway, dude tried to step and I told him if he ain't get out my fucking…oh, my bad…my face. I was gon' break'em up. Then Mom got all mad and told me she wasn't having all this mess in her house and so I was like 'fine, be like that dat. Take his side over some bullshit. I'm out!" So I bounced and now I'm over my girl's house," Ty explained.

"That's it! I'm going over there. This mess has got to stop. I ain't letting this get out of hand. I'll beep you later on and let you know when I get to Philly. Enough is enough. I'm going to have to handle this. I see I'm going to have to resort to my old ways," I responded angrily.

"What you gon' do?"

"First of all. You're just going to have to stay with me for a while. Malik too."

"Tay, I can't stay with you. I got a job now. I ain't coming all the way out to no Delaware. I'm a man now. I can handle mine and that punk-ass Winston."

"No, you're right. I keep forgetting that you're 21 now. I just don't want you to feel like you don't have a place to stay. I know Malik is not going to want to stay with me. He worships his father. Winston can't do any wrong in his eyes. He's too young to remember all the crap his father put this family through."

"Don't go over there tonight. I gotta work. Let's meet over there tomorrow night," Ty suggested.

"I gotta move on this thing now. But again, you're right. I need to calm down first," I replied.
I talked to my brother for a while and then we made our plan. We decided to meet over at my mom's house Friday night to try to explain to my mother the danger our family was in.

Only Fools Gamble Twice

Friday after work, I beeped Ty two times. The second time he called me back and said that he was called in to work. He explained that since this was a new job, he didn't want to mess up. I promised him that I wouldn't go over to my mom's without him. I thought about things more carefully, and I decided that my mother and I could talk one on one. I thought this was a good idea because I didn't want her to think that Ty and I were double-teaming her.

When I arrived at my mom's house that evening, Malik was playing with his friends on his scooter out front.

"Hey, big head," I said as I grabbed Malik in a head lock.

"Can I have some money?" he asked, holding out his hand. I pulled out a dollar bill and gave him the money.

"A dollar? What you think I'm gonna buy for a dollar?" he asked.

"Boy, you better take this dollar or get out of my face. Try getting a job. Next year you'll be fourteen. When I was your age I already had two jobs. Mommy in the house?" I asked.

"Yeah," Malik said as he climbed back on his scooter and headed to the store.

I tried opening the door, but it was locked. I rang the doorbell, not feeling like looking for my key. Winston appeared shirtless at the door and for a minute I thought I was going to throw up. It had been so long since I had seen him and I had forgotten how evilness looked so up close and personal.

I said nothing to him. I simply pushed by him to enter my home away from home, the house that I grew up in. Here was an evil spirit answering my mother's door.

As I entered the kitchen. I couldn't help but notice that mom was frying chicken and on the table were two cans of beer.

"Hey, Mom."

"Hey, baby," Mom slurred.

"Mom, have you been drinking?"

"Taylor! Don't start. I'm the mother here. If you're coming to start your mess, you can just leave now. I ain't for this shit tonight."

I almost fell over. My mother hadn't had a drink or used profanity in more than ten years. I couldn't understand what was going on.

Just then, Winston walked in the kitchen with this smirk on his face. "Hey, Barb. You need me to fold up those clothes upstairs on the bed?" he asked my mom as he placed his arms around her waist.

"Yeah. After that, I need you to take out the trash and clean the bathroom too."

"Oh, so now I'm just your house bitch, huh?" Winston asked as he laughed and slapped my mother on the butt.

You couldn't tell me I wasn't going to throw up my lunch. He then walked past me and winked, like he had gotten over on me.

"Baby girl, you looking good," he slurred, placing his arm on my shoulder.

Before I knew it I had jumped on his back, just punching him and slapping him upside his head. "You black motherfucker. I hate you! I hate you! You ain't nothing but a fucking pussy. Just get the fuck out! GET OUT, BITCH!" I screamed at the top of my lungs.

Only Fools Gamble Twice

Everything that I had been suppressing all week finally came pouring out. My mother pulled me off Winston and forcefully pushed me into a corner. "No, you get the fuck out! You ain't gon' be running my man out! If anybody leaves, it'll be you. I done got rid of your brother and you don't live here, so get out! Ya'll don't know what I got to go through here.

You got your fancy friends and your brother is always in that girl's face and who do I have, huh? Winston loves me and I love him and y'all all can kiss my ass."

It felt like someone had smacked me and taped my mouth shut. I was completely frozen and couldn't utter a word. I just stood there as the tears began to fall uncontrollably down my face. I don't remember what happened next, I just know through the grace of God I made it home safely.

As I picked up the phone to call Morgan, I heard a man's voice on the line.

"Taylor?"

"Yeah, what?" I asked angrily.

"Taylor, it's Delaney. Are you okay?"

"No, actually I'm not okay," I responded, beginning to realize just how nasty I was being.

"What's the matter? I've been calling you since Wednesday night. I was beginning to get worried."

"I'm having a very serious family crisis," I said as the tears began to fall from my swollen eyes.

"Can I come over?"

"No! I just want to be left alone," I said as I began crying uncontrollably.

"I'm sorry. I just can't do that. I'm on my way!" Delaney stated. He hung up the phone before I could protest.

Part of me wanted his company, but then the other part of me knew that there was no way that I would be feeling like my old self anytime in the future. I just wanted to be left alone. Besides, I looked like hell.

When Delaney arrived, I opened the door slowly and he came busting through the door like he had run all the way over to my house. He led me to my couch and he just held me tightly as I cried until my eyes were sore and dry. He didn't say a word, he just held me tightly and rocked me.

"Do you want to talk about it?" he asked softly.

"I just...I just don't know what the hell is going on," I began.

"You know what? Let's not talk about it. I know exactly what you need," Delaney said as he gently lifted my head from his shoulder and laid it down on the sofa.

He got up and went upstairs. I couldn't possibly imagine what he was doing and I didn't even care. I must have fallen asleep for about an hour because Delaney woke me up. It felt like my mind was wandering the entire time I was asleep.

"Come with me," he said as he pulled me from the sofa and led me upstairs to the bathroom.

When I opened the door, there were lit candles all over the room with my favorite song playing in the background.

"I'm going to run out and get a few things. I want you to take a bath and just relax. Try not to think about your problems, just soak, listen to the music, and I'll be back. If I'm not back in an hour, just try to get some sleep and I'll call you when I'm on my way," Delaney said, kissing me on my forehead and left before I could object.

As much as I tried to enjoy the bath Delaney had prepared for me, I just couldn't help but to relive everything that had gone wrong The phone rang and I thought of answering it, but I just didn't feel like talking to anyone. I figured if it were Delaney than he would just come back over. Let the voice mail pick it up.

After I tried and tried to relax, nothing seemed to work. I lay down on the couch and finally dozed off.   My phone rang and this time I figured I'd answer it.

"Hey, girl, what's up?" Morgan asked a little too perky for me.

"Girl, everything. My life is so fucked up right now,"

"Oh my goodness. Was that a curse word you just used in the name of Jesus?"

"I ain't for your shit. Yeah, it was a curse word. I feel like my life is a fucking curse at this moment."

"What the hell is going on? Are you okay?" Morgan asked, now obviously becoming concerned.

"My mom and her no-good ex-husband. Girl, you missed the drama that's been going on."

"Not Winston. He's back?"

"Yeah. The bastard's back on the scene now,"

"Get the hell out of here. Isn't that the guy who had your mom all fucked up before and now she's back with him?"

"I guess it's true that misery loves company. He probably just got out of rehab or jail or something and needed a place to stay. I just can't believe my mom fell for that dumb shit," I replied. I filled Morgan in on what went down and she was just as baffled as I was.

"Girl, if you need me, I'm here for you," Morgan said.

"I know. Right now, I just need peace and quiet. Delaney came over earlier and ran a bath for me and told me he'd be back soon. I'm supposed to be resting. You should see my damn eyes. They're swollen shut. Hold on, that's my other line," I stated and I clicked over to answer the phone.

"Hey, sweetness. It's me. I'm on my way. You feel any better? Were you able to rest?"

"Not really," I replied sadly.

"I know you want to be left alone, but I just don't think it's a good idea. I'm coming to get you in a few minutes. Can you pack some things? I want to take you away for the weekend."

"I really don't think I feel up to it," I protested.

"Please. I promise I'll give you your space. I just don't want you to be alone."

"Alright. Maybe getting away from all this drama is what I need."

"I'll see you in a few minutes."

"Peace."

I clicked back on the other line and explained to Morgan that I had to go and pack.

"Pack? Where are you going?" Morgan demanded.

"Delaney's taking me away for the weekend. I think this is just what the doctor ordered. I'm tired of worrying about everything and everybody. It's time I stop living my life for a bunch of damn adults and do what makes me happy. If my mom is being a fool than I have to wait until she can realize it for herself. She's a grown damn woman and she can definitely fend for herself. I gotta live for me," I declared.

"I know that's right. Just be there for her, but for now you just go and have some fun. Try not to think of things too much. I'll pray for your mom. 'Cause Lord knows she needs it now more than ever. Where is Delaney taking you anyway?"

"I don't know and I really don't care. I just don't want to have to make any decisions. I just wanna sit back, relax, and enjoy the damn ride. I gotta go, girl. I'll holla at you later on."

"Okay sista-friend. Don't forget, if you need me you know I'm here for you."

"You don't have to tell me that. If I don't know anything else, I know that."

After Morgan and I finished our conversation, I quickly pulled my hair into a tight ponytail and wet-set the ends. I showered and then decided what to wear. I didn't know if Delaney and I were doing something relaxing or going somewhere that would require me to dress nicely so I decided to wear a pair of red capri's and a red tank top. I put on my three-inch sandals, and packed a light knapsack with three extra outfits and a bikini just in case we were going to a place where there was a pool or something. I fed the animal kingdom, giving them enough food to last a lifetime.

Delaney arrived back at my house around 3:00 P.M. and he looked gorgeous as usual in a pair of denim shorts, a tank top, and a pair of sandals. I especially liked the tank top because it showed his perfectly sculpted biceps and pecks.

"Hey, sweetness. Come here, girl. You look beautiful as usual. You ready to head out?" he asked, gently kissing me on the lips and squeezing me tightly.

"Let me get my sunglasses. I know my eyes look like hell."

"They look good to me."

"Hey, listen, I didn't know where we were going so I hope that I'll be dressed appropriately," I said.

"Naw, you're cool. I know you're not up for a whole lot. This weekend is all about you and all about you relaxing. Understood?"

"I think I can manage that."

We climbed into Delaney's SUV and made our way to I-95 to get on the expressway.

"So are you ready to tell me where we're going?" I asked.

"Somewhere where there's plenty of relaxation going on and all that is required of you is to think about you and only you and to clear your mind of all your troubles. I think we're going to have a nice little trip," Delaney responded, pressing on the gas pedal.

Once we reached the New Jersey state line, I had a hunch that Delaney and I were headed to the Jersey shore. I remembered he said that he wanted to take me the following week, but I figured he must have made arrangements for us to go a week earlier since I was going through all this drama.

About an hour later, Delaney took the exit for the Atlantic City Expressway and my hunch was confirmed. When we arrived at the shore house in Cape May, New Jersey, I was pleasantly surprised. Although I'd been in Atlantic City about a dozen times, I'd never actually stayed over in Cape May.

We walked inside and the place was simply gorgeous. It was a huge home equipped with a fireplace in the living room, five bedrooms, a huge kitchen, four bathrooms, a deck with a Jacuzzi out back, and the Atlantic Ocean at our toes in the front of the beach house. I was in love--partly with Delaney for bringing me here and partly because I desperately needed this time to heal my soul. Work was stressful and now dealing with my problems at home seemed as if things were only going to get worse.

"Have you ever been to Cape May?" Delaney asked nervously.

"No, I've never been here."

"Well, there are five bedrooms here. Pick out the one you want and try to relax. I'll be back later," Delaney said, heading for the door.

"Where are you going?"

"I know you need some time to yourself. I'm going to take a drive, then maybe head over to Atlantic City and do some gambling."

"I wanna go. You can't just leave me here all alone." I said, pouting.

"I just thought you'd want to relax."

"You said this trip was all about me and I want to be with you. Besides, I wanna win some money. I've got plenty of time to relax later on. Let's go," I said, heading after him, trying my best to not think about my problems.

"We can do something else. There are tons of things we can do here other than gamble," Delaney said.

"Nope. A.C.'s fine."

When we arrived at the casino, we both decided that we wanted to walk the boardwalk before we let Trump win all of our money. We stayed on the boardwalk for about two hours, going into different shops and purchasing things neither of us needed like sunglasses, key chains, and T-shirts and even stopping for pizza. It was then that I remembered that I hadn't eaten in about a day and a half.

We decided to go to the carnival and Delaney and I both realized we loved the outrageous roller coasters and wild rides. By the time we left it was about nine o'clock and we decided to head to some of the casinos. We walked back up the beach in our bare feet, often stopping to sit and just watch the waves crashing. The cool saltwater breeze felt good against my skin, and I noticed that I had goose bumps. At that moment, I was so thankful for Delaney coming into my life. He was truly a life saver, rescuing me from thinking about the whole nonsense with my family. I was also thankful that he hadn't asked me the entire time about what had been going on. I couldn't tell if my goose bumps were from the breeze or the feeling of Delaney's arm wrapped tightly around my shoulders. All I knew is that I felt good for the first time in a few days.

Only Fools Gamble Twice

We went to one of the smaller casinos and since I am no gambler, I made it a point to spend no more than fifty dollars in any casino. I flagged down the cash attendant and she gave me change for my first twenty dollars. Delaney gave me a kiss on the lips and pointed to the blackjack table where he was headed.

"Where are you going?" he asked.

"I'll be over at the slot machines. I don't do that hardcore gambling," I said.

"You need any money?" he asked before he walked off.

"No, I'm cool. Thanks for asking. I'll be over in a little bit after I lose my money," I said.

"Now see you can't think like that. You have to think positive. Give me one of those good-luck kisses again," Delaney said, kissing me gently on the lips, squeezing my hand, then headed off to the blackjack table.

I tried for about twenty minutes to get on one of the nickel machines, but the senior citizen folks had the slots sewn up. Most of the seniors don't have anything to do with their time, so they get to the casinos early in the A.M. and don't leave until the wee hours of the morning. Reluctantly, I tried the quarter slots. I dropped my first quarter in and eighty quarters fell out. I continued to play and each time anywhere from ten to eighty quarters would drop out. After about ten minutes the machine started slowing up on my winnings and not being a true gambler, I grabbed a bucket and placed my winnings in it.

Only Fools Gamble Twice

There was an elderly lady who damn near knocked me down to get to the machine I had been on, but I just sucked my teeth and continued to walk on. I thought that there was no sense in getting upset, this place was probably her whole life. I cashed in my winnings and was surprised to learn that I had won $125. That was cool with me, and I wasn't about to lose it. I thanked the cashier, and then set out to find my sweetie. I found him at a nearby blackjack table, and from the looks of things, he didn't look too pleased.

"Hey, sweetie, what's your phone number?" I asked as I slipped my arm around Delaney's waist.

"Hey, sweetness, I ain't doin' too good. I've lost three hundred already. Can you believe that?" he asked, turning to look at me.

"You better not lose all of your money. I still haven't eaten yet, man," I teased.

"Yeah, I think I better quit before I lose my shirt," he stated dryly.

"Now I would be willing to bet that wouldn't be such a bad sight," I teased as I held out a ten-dollar bill and ran it slowly across his hug biceps. "C'mon, man. I'm hungry. I'll buy dinner."

"I'm out. I don't even think I can afford to pay the toll," he joked.

Delaney excused himself from the table and stretched out his long legs. He put his hand around my waist and guided me to the casino elevator. He leaned over and spoke closely to my ear. "My baby feeling any better?" he asked.

"Much. I want to thank you for bringing me here. I really needed to get away."

"The pleasure's all mine. Anything for my sweetness. Check this out. They have this restaurant upstairs that has really good food. I hope you're hungry. I'm starving and right about now you look good enough to eat," Delaney stated.

To be honest I couldn't tell if he was flirting or if he just happened to be speaking so closely to my ear. At any rate, I couldn't blame him because with all the stress that I was going through, I was definitely going to be relieving some later on. I jerked my head away and instantly started to blush. "Yeah, I'm pretty hungry too. All I had today was that pizza from the boardwalk. I haven't eaten since yesterday morning," I said.

"That's no good. Let's hope this restaurant is open so we can feed my sweetness."

We arrived at the restaurant and were seated immediately by the waitress. It was one of those twenty-four-hour places that served breakfast, lunch, and dinner. I was in the mood for pancakes so I ordered an egg-and-cheese omelet with a side order of pancakes. Delaney ordered the baked chicken, vegetables, and a baked potato. While we waited for our food, I figured now was a good time to fill Delaney in on my family drama.

When I finished my story, Delaney looked like he wanted to explode.

"Why didn't you tell me this before we left? I'm ready to go over there and squash homie. I want to meet this joker. He needs to be confronted by a man," Delaney said, his eyes about to bulge from their sockets. "I can't believe this shit. Excuse me for cursing but that kind of shit really pisses me off!"

"I don't want you to get involved. The way that I'm going to handle this is I just won't go over to my mom's house anytime soon. I'm angrier at her for talking to me the way she did. She kicked me out."

"Taylor, I'm not taking up for your moms, but she was probably torn between you and him. I'm pissed that this guy, who calls himself a man, stepped to you like that. I want to meet this asshole. Let him step up in my face like that!" he responded.

"You know what, we were having a good time before all of this. It took me damn near all day to not think about things, and I don't want to ruin my evening with you talking about something we have no control over," I replied.

Just then our food came and I was relieved we didn't have to talk about it anymore. Delaney still seemed pissed, but he gave me one of those looks that told me this was not the end of things but that he also wouldn't ruin our weekend together.

I guess we hadn't realized we were that hungry because we ate everything in sight including dessert. After we ate, I tried to convince Delaney to let me pay for dinner, but he wouldn't hear of it. I figured since he lost his money and I had won so much, I could help a brother out. Delaney being a complete gentleman, wouldn't hear it. But I insisted, and he resisted, so I convinced him to allow me to leave the tip. I left a more than generous one, and we headed back to the shore house.

We got back around 11:30 and Delaney suggested that we change clothes. I ran a shower and couldn't help but allow yesterday's thoughts to creep into my mind. I quickly dismissed them and recalled the wonderful day that Delaney and I shared. I changed into my neon green silk sarong and a matching bikini. I knew this outfit was quite revealing, but I wanted it to be that way. I wanted to walk on the wild side. I was tired of being good ole Taylor. The church girl. The girl who didn't curse and considered everyone's feelings. What about me? Yeah, my mother had needs, but so did I. It was time for me to get what I could and be damn happy about it.

I wanted to surprise Delaney, so I put on my silk robe. When I came downstairs, Delaney had the fireplace and warm jazz going. The mood was set, and like Emeril the chef says, I was going to kick it up a notch! I searched for Delaney and found him out on the deck in the Jacuzzi. Perfect place to make my move.

"You didn't tell me to bring my bathing suit," I said seductively, walking toward him.

"My bad, I forgot to remind you. I'll be inside in a minute. I just wanted to soak my aching muscles. I ran yesterday and I'm still pretty sore. Go in and have a seat, I have some Zinfandel chilling, go get a drink and make yourself comfortable," Delaney said.

I dropped my robe and I knew from the way that he was checking me out that he was more than pleased at what I was wearing.

I continued to stand there and then slowly, very slowly I untied the sarong and revealed my matching bikini thong. I then began walking toward him and carefully stepped in the warm water. I walked over to him and straddled him.

"You don't mind if I join you, do you?"

"Damn. You sure know how to turn the heat up, don't you?" he said as he placed his arms around my waist and then began kissing me like I was the first woman he had seen after being on lock down for fifty years.

I abruptly stopped kissing him and then looked deeply into his eyes. Feeling his arousal made me experience a connection with him. It was something that I couldn't ever remember experiencing. Besides that, it had been two years since I had even been remotely close to any man. I slowly bent my head and we had the most animalistic kiss I had ever experienced.

Delaney suddenly stopped. "Taylor?" he whispered.

"What did you call me? I'm not sweetness anymore?" I asked seductively as I poked out my bottom lip teasingly.

Delaney pulled me tighter. Our bodies locked and our mouths probed each other. At that moment, I was completely in control of where I wanted things to go.

I nibbled on his bottom lip and then began placing light, gentle kisses all over his face. I kissed his nose, his eyes, and then I moved around to his ear. Delaney let out a light moan when I reached his ear. I began to breathe heavily into it and then I began to gently lick the outside perimeter, down to his earlobe. Delaney grabbed my shoulders and again, suddenly stopped kissing me and let out a low grunt.

"Woman, you're on shaky ground. You know that's the danger zone. You don't want to mess with that," Delaney cautioned.

"Tell me, do I still have my position as sweetness?" I asked seductively.

"Does this answer it for you?" Delaney asked as he cupped my breasts, pulling gently at my nipples through the flimsy material.

He slowly unfastened my bikini top, exposing my medium-sized breasts. He took each of them in his large hands and massaged them like he was a masseuse. It felt totally invigorating. He than began licking them gently as I made soft pleas for him to stop. He was driving me wild. He then moved his strong lips to mine and his tongue prodded my mouth. He then placed wet kisses on my face. He gently pushed my neck back and ran his tongue up and down it and then around the back. Still on his lap, I began moving up, down, and to the side. Delaney tugged at my face and then began to lightly blow in my ear, now violating my danger zone. He pushed his tongue in my ear and it was now my turn to let out a light gasp.

"Sweetness, I want you so badly. I think we'd better stop."

I abruptly stopped kissing him and asked, "Why? We're both adults. I want you, Delaney," I said as I began kissing him again.

He stopped kissing me yet again.

"I know you're going through some hard times with your family. I just want to be sure this is what you want and you're not trying to escape to a place that will take your mind off your troubles."

"I'm not using you if that's what you're thinking. I know what I'm doing and I also know that I want you. I wanted you the first night we met, but experience has taught me not to want you so badly. I also know that you're talking way too much. Now shut up and kiss me, please," I said as Delaney grabbed my shoulders and kissed me like he was auditioning for the lead part as the man in my life. Little did he know he already had the part and was up for an Emmy in my book.

"Like I said earlier, this entire day is all about you. I wanna make you feel good. We have some unfinished business to tend to. Let's get out of this damn Jacuzzi." He carefully led me out of the huge tub and upstairs dripping water all throughout the house but we had only one care in the world and that was pleasing each other.

When we arrived at the master bedroom, Delaney grabbed two towels, placing one around his waist as he delicately removed my wet thong. He dried me off, ensuring that he'd gotten every spot.

He wrapped my towel around me and whispered in my ear, directing me to the huge king-sized bed. "I want every inch of you to be dry because I want to make you wet all over."

"I don't think you're going to have to worry about that. I'm wet enough to call off a summer drought in Sahara," I said, allowing myself to seize the moment that I never wanted to end.

Delaney suddenly turned around and unfastened both of our towels. He gently stroked my clitoris and I thought I would explode.

"Damn, sweetness. You really are wet, baby" He stood playing with my womanhood, which was begging for more. He then flipped the danger zone move on me yet again and started to lick and nibble on my ear. I let out a light yelp as I allowed my body to become limp from the heated climax he brought me to. Afterward, I pushed him on the bed gently, then headed back to my overnight bag, where I retrieved a female condom. I cleansed myself and then headed back to the bed.

"What's that?" he asked with a puzzled look on his face.

"A female condom. My gynecologist gave me a ton of these. She swears by them. I've never used one, but I hear they're supposed to be really good."

Delaney and I continued to explore each other and our bodies screamed for fulfillment. His huge hands placing the female condom inside of me caused me to have another climax. Delaney became so excited from helping me with the device, he nearly climaxed too. When he entered me, I wrapped my legs around his waist and pressed on his back, demanding more of his manhood.

"Damn, sweetness, you're so tight. I'm trying to hold on, but it's just soooo good," he said, moaning.

I thrust my hips harder and before I knew it, I had brought him to a climax of his very own.

"Whew, that ain't fair. Why did you do that to me? You made me a two-hump chump," Delaney said, his breathing still hot and heavy. We both laughed and I promised him that I had more female condoms and we had all the time in the world to use as many as we liked.

8/MORGAN

The week I had at work proved to be more stressful than I had ever imagined. On Wednesday, Rhonda didn't show up until ten. She hadn't bothered to call to say that she would be late or anything. She just casually strolled in, caught my eye, and began her duties. I called her to my office and told her that her services were no longer needed. I didn't have time for the bullshit. If she didn't want to work, I would find someone who did.

    Of course Rhonda didn't leave without much chaos. She had the nerve to threaten to kick my ass the next time she saw me. *Oh, I was really scared. Imagine that!* I was about to go DMX on her ass, but I was up in there, up in there, so I played the part of a true business professional and called security to have her forcibly removed from the premises. It was truly embarrassing to see a grown woman stoop so low. In the end, things actually worked out. Cheryl from human resources called me later that afternoon to let me know she had an elderly woman on the employment waiting list. Apparently there was a woman who used to work for the company and now wanted to return. I told Cheryl to hire the woman and that was all she wrote. I didn't have time to train someone fully, so this would be great for each of us. The woman told Cheryl she could start the following day, which was really good news to me. I stopped by my parents' house on Wednesday and my mom told me that she hadn't been feeling well. Her skin looked a little ashened and she looked like she had dropped more weight. She told me not to worry, then cooked me one of my favorite meals, which consisted of fried chicken, baked macaroni and cheese, and fresh collard greens.

My dad looked worried, but each time I tried to persist, they clammed up. I knew something was up but they didn't want to talk about it, so I just pushed the thoughts out of my mind and figured it was fatigue or something.

My parents had been married for so long, and I secretly wished that one day I would find me a mate who would love me the way my father loved my mother. My dad was a good-looking man, in his mid-fifties and my mother was a true beauty. Together, they made the picture-perfect couple.

My mom and dad have always talked about the day when they could retire. My dad had recently decided that he was going to retire at fifty-seven which was just four years away. My mother on the other hand is only fifty and she was going to retire with my dad. My parents have each worked so hard all of their lives to provide for my older sister and me that I just wanted them to sit back, relax, and enjoy their lives together, you know, travel to places unknown. I've seen people work half of their lives saving money and never enjoying life, only to die before they ever have a chance to live how they wanted to live.

By the time Thursday rolled around I had spoken to Kofie about two times in the evening. He seemed like an extremely intelligent man and I was looking forward to having dinner and drinks with him. We decided to meet at Savannah's, a local club and restaurant on Callowhill Street, which had a live jazz band playing that evening.

"Hi, I'm not late, am I?" I asked Kofie as the hostess showed me to the table.

"No, I made it a point to arrive early. I wanted to make sure we had a good table," Kofie said. He flashed his bright smile, which displayed the large gap in his front teeth. He handed me a menu, which had all of my favorite foods. It was going to be difficult deciding what I wanted to eat.

"I hope you don't mind, I ordered a bottle of Cristal for us," Kofie stated.

"Yeah, that's cool, Cris is pretty good," I lied. Actually I didn't particularly care for the stuff. I personally liked white wines, but I would drink it anyway. I am not accustomed to men making decisions for me, but I figured that since I was so head-strong, it was just me being me.

"Hi, I'm Adrianne, your waitress for the evening. Would you like to hear the specials or are you to ready to order?" The waitress asked.

"Yes, we are. The lady will have the grilled salmon and I'll have the steamed shrimp," now I was beginning to get really pissed. I had just arrived and didn't really get a good chance to look at the menu. It was a long day. I had to make myself calm down.

"I'll have the Cajun chicken salad please and a glass of water with lemon," I said as I closed the menu and returned it to the waitress.

"Please bring bread and extra butter with that," Kofie said, handing the waitress his menu.

"No problem. Your order will be ready shortly," the waitress said as she took the menu and walked away.

"So, how was your day?" Kofie asked.

"It wasn't so bad. My new assistant started. I think she's

going to work out just fine. She worked there about a year ago and then left because her husband was sick. He recently died, so she decided to come back to work. The beginning part of my week was a little hectic, though," I said, leaning back in my chair.

"What was so hectic about it?" Kofie asked in his heavy accent.

I explained the entire situation with Rhonda to Kofie and how I had just earned a promotion. "It'll be longer hours and more stress, but I think I'm ready for the challenge. As long as I have a good assistant, I think I'll be alright," I explained.

"Sounds like you'll be as busy as me. With all of the projects I have going, sometimes I don't know if I'm coming or going." Kofie laughed.

The waitress brought our food and while we ate we enjoyed the smooth sounds of the local jazz band.

After dinner, Kofie suggested that we drive to Penns Landing to go for a walk. I looked at my watch and realized it was nine o'clock.

"I think I had better decline Kofie. I have to get up early tomorrow and there is a stack of work on my desk at home that I should tackle tonight. How about sometime next weekend we can get together?" I asked.

"Next weekend is no good for me. I'll be in New York checking on my other projects. How about next Thursday? Same time, same place?" Kofie suggested.

I hurriedly pulled out my day planner and realized that I would be out of town next week, at our satellite office.

"I'm in New York next week. I'm afraid I can't make it.

Only Fools Gamble Twice

I'll call you and we can arrange something after next weekend," I promised.

"Since you're going to be in New York during the week and I'll be there on the weekend, perhaps I can come up a day early and we can get together there. What do you say?" Kofie suggested.

"I know I'll be pretty busy while I'm up there, but I'll let you know," I replied, not really sure what I thought about that idea.

Kofie paid the waitress and left a sizable tip. I had parked around the corner, and as it turned out Kofie had parked in the same lot. Kofie shook my hand, which I thought was a bit conservative. It seemed more like a business date than anything else.

"I thank you for spending your evening with me," Kofie said.

"Thank you for dinner. I had a really nice time. How about next time, dinner is on me?" I suggested.

"I won't hear of it. I know that you're an independent woman, but as long as you're with me you don't have to worry about money or picking up any bills," Kofie replied confidently.

We said good night and then Kofie showed me to my car, closed the door and waited until I had locked it and started up the engine. I watched Kofie as he walked to his car, and then waved when he got in. I exited the parking lot and headed back to Delaware.

I reflected on the evening with Kofie. He seemed really nice and was definitely a gentleman, but he seemed like he was holding back. Like there was a wall that you couldn't penetrate.

For now though, it was nice to meet a man and not have to worry about him pawing me half to death and then trying to get into your pocket to pay for any and everything. I just wasn't sure how I felt about him. I'd see how things turn out.

When I got home, I had two messages--one from Mister and one from Carla, my sorority sister.

I knew Carla was probably upset because I still hadn't gotten over to her new club. I had to make sure that I placed that on my list of priorities.

Mister was calling to invite me to Sonny's the following evening. There was no way I'd be going anywhere with him.

I called Carla and promised her that I'd be over to her club the following evening. We talked about our last sorority meeting and the possibility of a new line for membership intake and about some of our old friends. I knew that I had tons of work to complete so I hurriedly got off the phone with her so I could meet my deadlines.

I cleared the messages, grabbed a small bottle of Verdi out of the fridge and headed to my second bedroom, which I had converted into an office. I thumbed through the stack of work and began the tedious task at hand. Around midnight I decided that I had completed about as much work as humanly possible. In all actuality, I had gotten more work done at home than I could have done in one week at the office. It was nice not to be bothered and interrupted to answer phone calls or have people constantly stopping by your desk to chat about their personal issues.

I arrived at work around seven on Friday morning and was amazed to see my assistant, Henrietta, already hard at work.

"Good morning, Ms. Watson," Henrietta said in her perky morning voice.

"Henrietta, please just call me Morgan

"Now you never mind, young lady. That's the way I was raised. Anyone who's in charge of your money goes by Mr. or Ms. How about I call you Morgan in the office, but if some big shot is around, I'll call you Ms. Watson?" Henrietta suggested.

"Only if you'll allow me to do the same," I responded.

"Than it's a deal," Henrietta said as she clasped her hands together.

"How long have you been here? It's pretty early," I said, looking at my watch.

"Oh, I've been here since six," Henrietta said.

"Six? I think I've finally hit the jackpot," I said, looking amazed.

"Heavens. Why do you say that?" Henrietta looked startled.

"Let's just say my last assistant didn't bother to show up until mid-morning," I said as I headed for my cubicle.

"I've never heard of such a thing. Ever since my husband, Wilbur, passed, God bless his soul, I don't sleep much. I figure instead of me laying around getting all depressed, I can get up and go to work. There's always work to be done. So I either get up to clean or do a crossword puzzle. Now that I have a job, there's no reason why I can't be productive here," Henrietta said, displaying her bright white dentures.

"Well let's just say that I'm glad you're here. I think we're going to get along just fine," I said, reaching my cubicle.

As I sat down, I smiled to myself. Things were going

Only Fools Gamble Twice

great. I was pleased when Cheryl from HR brought Henrietta down to my cubicle. When Cheryl first told me they hired a Henrietta McNeill, I instantly assumed that she would be an older white woman, based on her name. But when I saw the black woman walking toward me all tall and proud, I thought I would scream. We didn't have many people of color at Beckerman and Leechum and when Rhonda had displayed her ignorance, I was disappointed. In my opinion, all of us Blacks at Beckerman and Leechum were on public display and we were representing for our people. At any rate, I was happy to see a sista get another sista a chance in the growing company.

    Although the work was flowing more than usual, Henrietta and I were holding it down. With me being able to concentrate on the accounts I had lined up, Henrietta took care of all of the administrative work. When a client would phone in, before Henrietta would put him through, she would e-mail me his account profile. By the time I had picked up on the phone line, the account was available, which saved me time. When I would hang up with the client, Henrietta was right at my door inquiring about what was needed on her part. Life couldn't get any better, I thought. By the time lunch rolled around, I demanded that Henrietta take the time to relax. She protested at first, but then went away reluctantly. I wasn't really hungry so I went to the vending machine and grabbed a bag of popcorn and an apple juice.

    When I returned to my desk, I noticed that I had a message on my voice mail. It was from Sharon the receptionist telling me I had a package at the front desk. I opted to go pick it up myself. Knowing the mail carrier, Rudy, there was no telling when he would deliver it. When I arrived at the lobby, I saw a

Only Fools Gamble Twice

bouquet of roses and a dessert basket.

"Hi, Morgan. Both of these came for you within five minutes of each other," Sharon stated with a smirk. Sharon prided herself on knowing everyone's business in the company. As I picked up the huge packages, I thanked Sharon and began to walk away.

"You're not going to open the cards here?" Sharon inquired, looking upset.

"No, thank you," I said as I turned on my heel.

I knew Sharon would call everyone she could think of to try to investigate the matter, but as far as I was concerned it just wasn't any of her business. As I walked back to my desk, I couldn't figure out who'd sent the gifts. When I was safely in my office, I carefully set the vase of flowers and the fruit basket down and tore open the first small envelope.

It read:

I am probably one of the dumbest dummies in the world. We really need to talk. So much has changed in my life. I am nothing without you.

Love,

Mister

That was a first. Mister sending me roses and a gift basket, too, was more than I could handle. I tore open the second envelope and it read:

Friends are like roses in the garden of life. I look forward to hopefully seeing you next week.

Thinking of you,

Kofie.

Well that surely threw me for a loop. Not only was Kofie

a gentleman, but he was a generous one too. This was the second time he'd sent me a gift within the last week.

I knew Mister was trying to get me back so he sent the roses, but I had just met Kofie and that was one of the nicest things anyone had done for me. Just as I reached for the phone, it rang.

"Did you receive a package?" Kofie's deep accent flooded the phone.

"As a matter of fact, I did. I just finished reading the card. Thank you so much, of course it looks delicious." I said softly into the receiver.

"I just wanted to thank you for the lovely evening we had last night. I really enjoyed myself. I am taking off for New York in about an hour and I just wanted to tell you to have a good weekend and don't have too much fun without me," Kofie laughed lightheartedly into the receiver.

"That goes double for you. Be safe and thank you again. That was very thoughtful of you," I said before we hung up the phone.

After hanging up the phone, I decided to e-mail Mister and thank him for sending me the roses. I just wasn't up for calling him.

After Henrietta returned from lunch she checked in with me, looked at the roses and gift basket and said nothing.

Henrietta and I continued to work feverishly until 6:30 when I finally demanded that we each go home. I was pleased because Bernie had come over to the unit quite a few times and commented on how pleased he was at my performance and how Henrietta was definitely working out at the company. I wished

Henrietta a good weekend and reminded her that I would be in New York the following week. I promised her that I'd check in and gave her the hotel number where I'd be staying. Henrietta wished me a good night and a great weekend.

I needed to complete one last assignment and I was heading home, grabbing a quick shower, and going over to the Butter Cup Lounge. Just as I was finishing up my assignment, the phone rang.

"I see you received the roses. You couldn't call me?" Mister stated, sadly.

"I was really busy. This phone has been ringing nonstop. I was going to call you a little later on," I lied.

"I know you're lying. I know you said you're really busy now with work, but don't lie and say you were going to call," he responded, becoming angry.

"So now *I'm* a liar. Have I ever lied to you?" I stated, becoming angry myself.

"Listen, I didn't call to argue you with you. I want to talk to you about what I wrote in the card. So much has changed in my life," Mister stated.

"Go ahead. Tell me what's on your mind."

"Can we meet over at Sonny's? I don't want to talk on the phone. Just to have one drink," he said.

"I can't. I have plans already."

"Oh. You have plans with that dude you were out with last night? Don't think I don't know your ass wasn't home until late last night," he stated angrily.

"Whom I have plans with is absolutely none of your business. If you haven't noticed, we are not together. You broke up with me. I'm not going to get into this with you. Not now, and definitely not at my job. I thought we were getting along much better, but I see ain't a damn thing changed. I gotta go," I stated, hanging up the phone in his ear.

When I arrived home, I noticed I had two messages and of course they were both from Mister. His ass was all apologetic. Said he was going to Sonny's after work and asked again if I'd meet him for a drink. Of course I wasn't going. He also told me he would be staying there until about 7:30 and to page him and maybe we could go out to dinner. Like hell I would.

I showered, changed into my little black dress, otherwise known as my fuck'em dress. I used to wear dresses like this when I wanted the world to KMA (kiss my ass) and that's exactly how I felt at the moment. Well, maybe not the entire world, just Mister. I looked at myself in the mirror, pulled my boobies up to make sure they received their own attention, sprayed my favorite perfume behind my ears, and behind my knee caps, examined myself at all angles, and just knew you couldn't tell me that I didn't look good.

I thought about calling Taylor, but then I remembered she had plans with Delaney and was going through all of that drama. I made a mental note to reach out to her to make sure she was okay.

I arrived at the Butter Cup Lounge and I was most definitely impressed. The place was magnificent. Courtney is an interior decorator, so I knew that she certainly put her thing down in here. It was majestic with black-and-gold decor. It had that earthy kind of feel, but I felt nice and comfortable. I flagged Carla down and she ran over and gave me a huge hug.

Only Fools Gamble Twice

"Girl, it's about time you brought your raggedy ass in here. I can't believe it took you this long," Carla yelled over the booming music.

"This place is nice. Where did you get those beige leather sofas?" I yelled.

"Girl, you know I got the hookup. Come on. The first two drinks are on me then you're on your own," Carla said, pulling me to the VIP section.

When we got there, I greeted a few people I knew. I saw two of my sorors who were with their husbands, and I greeted them and sat at a nearby table with Carla and her business partner Lisa.

As quiet as it's kept, I think Carla and Lisa are more than just business partners, but I ain't one to gossip and you ain't heard that from me. Carla's my girl and I'll always love her for how she treats me and what she does in the privacy of her own home is her business.

Carla, Lisa, and I talked about how they came up with the idea for the Butter Cup Lounge and their plans to open up another lounge in Philly. They were currently looking for more investors and they made me a proposal that I had to contemplate further. All they needed was $3,500 and I would have a return of $7,000 within a month.

"Of course we don't expect an answer today. I wasn't even going to bring it up here, but since I never get a chance to see or hear from you, now is as good a time as any," Carla stated.

"Let me get back to you. I'll be in New York next week. When I get back, I should have a chance to go over my finances," I replied.

We continued to talk and I ordered some clams. Apparently, seafood was their specialty. As I waited for my food, Lisa excused herself and went to her office upstairs. I checked Lisa out and noticed how attractive she was and how Carla looked at her with only the pride your lover has when you walk away.

Carla and I continued to talk and then as if looking at the past walk in front of me, I noticed Mister walk up the stairs to the VIP section with his college roommate, Kevin.

I tried to act as if I didn't notice them, but it was too late. Mister started beaming and walked right over.

"What are you doing here? I thought you said you had plans," Mister said.

"Good to see you, Kevin. How have you been?" I asked, ignoring Mister's question.

"Good. I see you're looking as lovely as ever," Kevin said, with a raised eyebrow. "Carla, you're looking good too. This place is really nice. Congratulations are definitely in order," Kevin said, bending down to kiss Carla on her cheek.

"Thanks. It took a long time, but we're finally up and running. Can I get you guys anything to drink or eat?" Courtney asked.

"Yeah, I'll have a vodka and cranberry juice. You drinking the same, dawg?" Kevin asked, turning to Mister.

"Yeah, why not?" Mister stated, still staring at me, looking mad as all hell.

"Morg, what you drinking?" Kevin asked.

"I'm alright. I'm driving so I have to pace myself."

"Come on. How long has it been since we all hung out

together like the good ol' days? Have a drink with us. Please," Kevin begged.

Kevin was always my boy. Out of all the friends Mister had, he was the one who I always trusted and he was genuinely a nice guy. He's married with one son. A good father and husband to his wife.

"Fine! Just one. I'll drink what you're both drinking," I said, knowing good and well that I am no vodka drinker. That was my first mistake right there. I should have ordered my white wine and called it a night. Good thing my food came when it did. At least I wouldn't be sick.

Carla took their order than excused herself to go get our drinks.

"So you're not going to talk to me?" Mister asked, looking sad.

I ignored him and rolled my eyes. When, our drinks arrived a few minutes later, Kevin proposed a toast. "To a lifetime of friendship."

We each clinked glasses and Kevin and Mister downed their drinks. I sipped on mine because it was rather strong.

"Aw, come on, Morg. You gotta down that. You can't nurse that all night," Kevin protested.

"I'm a lady. We don't just down our drinks," I said mockingly as I held my hand to my chest.

"Well you stomping with the big dawgs tonight. Come on, down that thang," Kevin said.

"Naw, man, she can't hold her liquor like that," Mister challenged.

"What? What are you talking about? I know how to hold

my own," I replied, accepting the challenge like a homemade fool.

"Morgan, remember that time we went to Brave New World and we had those shots, and you threw up?" Mister reminded me.

"Yeah, you looked like the girl who was throwing up in the movie from the Sixth Sense. That shit was funny as hell," Kevin said.

"How could I forget? You all called me Six for the next few weeks? Besides, that was because I didn't have anything to eat. Don't worry, I got this," I responded as I downed my drink.

Before I knew it, Kevin was ordering another round. I tried to protest, but to no avail.

Don't ask me why or how, well we all know how, but those drinks started catching up to me, because before I knew it, I was laughing and dancing and sitting on Mister's lap. I don't think he was too drunk, but Kevin and I kept laughing, hugging, and everything was just so damn funny. Kevin and I were on the dance floor and we were cutting up. Mister came out there and whispered something in Kevin's ear and Kevin grabbed my hand, gave me a kiss on the cheek, and left the dance floor. Mister and I started dancing and before I knew what had come over me, I was leaning in and kissing Mister, right there on the dance floor.

"Come on, let me get you home. I don't believe Kevin did that shit. Sit right here, and I'll get Kevin and we can get out of here," Mister said, sitting me down and heading up to the VIP section to get Kevin.

"Hey, girl, did you have too much to drink?" Lisa asked, leaning down in my face.

"Hey, girl, where's my girl Carla?" I slurred.

"She's in the office. Did you drive?" Lisa asked.

"Yeah, but I'm in no condition to drive. Can I keep my car in your parking lot? I can catch a cab home," I said.

"I'll take your car to our house and you can call Carla in the morning and pick it up. Where are your keys?" Lisa asked in a concerned voice.

"Here! Ta da!" I said as I fished through my purse and found my keys. "You know what my car looks like?" I asked.

"Yeah. Let me get you some coffee," Lisa said, taking my car key and handing me back the rest of the keys.

"I don't drink coffee," I responded.

"Well you do now. I can't let you go like this," Lisa stated.

"I just need you to call me a cab. I'll be fine," I said.

Just then, Mister walked up with a drunken Kevin on his arm.

"Thanks, Lisa, I'm going to take them home. If you could just drop Morgan's car at her house and put her key in the door, she'll get them in the morning," Mister suggested.

"We were just discussing that. I'm going to take her car to our house and she can pick it up in the morning. Carla and I drove in one car and that won't be a problem. Why did you let them get like this?" Lisa asked Mister.

"These two are the most stubborn people I've ever met. Try telling either of them they can't do something and just watch what happens," Mister stated. "Come on, let me get you two home."

I waved good night to Carla and she came rushing over

and offered to let me stay with her. I just wanted to go home. We said good night again and Mister, Kevin, and I left the club.

Thankfully, Kevin lived just five minutes away, which was not out of the way from my home. I just wanted to get into my bed and go to sleep.

We dropped Kevin off. Mister made sure he was safely in and I waved a drunken good-bye to Kevin. I must have passed out, because what I remember is being carried out of the car to my town house by Mister.

"I'm okay. I'm okay! Stop fussing! Get your hands off of me," I demanded.

"I'm just trying to make sure you get in okay," Mister stated.

As I walked up to the door and searched for my house key, it took me longer than normal because I couldn't see or feel inside of my handbag.

As I tried to get my key into the door, I felt Mister's body press up against my back, reaching around me to help me with my keys.

Suddenly, I became so sexually aroused. Blame it on the liquor or what have you, but I needed him more than anything else at that very moment. I slowly began to purposely take forever to find my keys. I began moving my ass until I felt his erection.

"Stop it, Morgan. Don't play games with me. I know you're drunk and I'm not going out like this," Mister declared.

Still in the doorway, I then completely bent over and began wiggling up and down on his erection, which was now harder than I'd ever remembered.

I know Mister and when he and I were together, our sex life was off the hook! I knew he couldn't take it any longer and I also knew that he didn't want me to think he was taking advantage of me, but damn that, I needed me some--and bad!

Mister took the keys out of my hand and tried to find the one that would open the door.

"I don't know what kind of games you're playing, but you're not going to blame me in the morning for something you're going to regret. Now we're going to get you in the house and get you to bed and then I'm leaving and that's that!" Mister declared.

Right there in the doorway I began removing my dress. I said, "Look damn it, do you wanna fuck or not? We're not going to get back together or anything like that. I just wanna fuck and that's that! Nothing more, nothing less," I responded.

"Stop it, Morgan! Mister said, pulling my dress back on my shoulder. "See, that's the problem. I don't just wanna fuck you. I love you. Don't you see that? I want us to be an us, again," he said.

"Stop acting soft. Begging doesn't look good on you. You made your bed, now you lay in it. I don't have time for this mushy crap. I just want you to do me," I stated.

He then pushed me against the doorway and right there began grinding up and down my behind, up and down my back. Mister started to feel between my legs, grabbing and pulling on my little black dress, then suddenly he stopped and began feeling my breasts. He tugged at the material and then pulled one of my breasts out of the bra, pulling gently on my nipple. He turned me around and then forcefully ripped the sleeve off. Under normal circumstances I would have been upset because this fool was ripping my expensive little black dress. This wasn't no bargain outfit, but again, blame it on the alcohol.

    I was feeling so good and it had been so long since I had been on the verge of total and utter bliss that I nearly climaxed right there in the front of my house for all of the neighbors to see. Simply put, Mister is a great lover and knows exactly how to work his magic. More than likely he knew that he was the best lover that I'd ever had, but I sure as hell would never reveal that to him.

    "Hold on. I have to go to the bathroom," I whispered.

    "Come on, let's get inside of the house," he said as I moved out of his way and he opened the front door with my key. "Hurry back, baby," Mister whispered into my ear.

    I had to pee like a crazy woman--all that alcohol will do that to you.

    After I relieved myself, I quickly removed my clothes and then jumped into the shower. I was trying to wake the hell up and hopefully cool my hormones down, to no avail.

    Suddenly, I felt Mister slide his hard body up against mine in the shower. He took my washcloth and began to wash between my legs. It felt too good to be true. He washed my back, my neck, and even ran the cloth through my hair. He bent me over and washed my backside, legs, and my feet. This was the best washing I'd ever had. Mister then pushed me under the water and the soap cascaded over the length of my body. Next, he began gently kissing me all over before reaching the spot that he had visited so many times before. As the warm water continued to fall over my body, Mister's tongue entered the area he knew so well. I placed my leg on the shower seat and his tongue went even deeper. His tongue probed and my body quickly responded with the answer. He slowly bit my clitoris and I continued with explosion after explosion. After what seemed like invigorating pleasure, he removed his tongue and slowly allowed it to travel up my body.

I stepped out of the shower and allowed him to wash himself. I dried myself in the bathroom and slowly the effects of the alcohol were diminishing. I looked at myself in the mirror and wondered what I was doing. Getting my groove on with no strings attached? Men do it all the time. If I had my way, I was going to get a few more grooves on again this very night.

I got in the bed and must have dozed off. The next thing I know Mister's tongue was again deeply inside of me.

"You have the best stuff in the world. I always did love your goods," Mister said as he gently bit my clitoris again, sending me into oblivion.

He slowly opened the lips of my womanhood and passionately licked as if he were sucking a lollipop he was afraid would break if he was too rough. I let out a soft moan and knew that I was on the verge of yet another explosion. When he finally came up for air, I tried to kiss him on his chest but he pushed me lightly away.

"I've been a bad boy and I owe you this one. Just lay back and let me make you feel good," Mister whispered.

After my fifth orgasm, he began all over again. He ran his fingers through my wet hair, giving me a massage. He then left no area uncovered, kissing my eyes, ears, and even running his tongue up my nose. Mister has always been eccentric in the lovemaking department. He loved to smell my panties and seemed to get even more excited when they were dirty. In fact, the dirtier, the better they were for him. But he sure knew how to make me feel good and I had yet to find anyone who could come remotely close to him in this department. Mister began to suck my breasts, when suddenly the phone rang. As a reaction I reached for it. But was quickly distracted as Mister inched down my body kissing my navel and retreating to the place where he had given me so much pleasure so many times before. Mister brought me to a climax over and over for what seemed like hours. Our lovemaking had always been powerful, but I hadn't remembered it being like this. I must have drifted off to sleep but then I felt Mister gently kissing my back.

"Wake up, baby girl. You ain't that tired. I want to talk with you," Mister said as he turned me over to face him.

"What time is it?" I asked sleepily

"It's about 4:00 A.M." Mister replied as if he had been awake for hours. Mister got up from the bed and went into the living room for a moment. He came back a few seconds later and got back into the bed beside me.

"You know on that card I sent you, it said that that I wanted to talk to you about something."

"Yeah, but why choose now as the perfect opportunity to talk? It's 4:00. I'm tired as hell and you got the raps?" I asked as I turned over to regain my sleep.

"I just want to talk. I can't sleep. What do you think about us getting back together? Before you say anything, let me explain. I've really been going through it. When we were engaged, I wanted nothing more than to get married. But then I realized that I wasn't ready. Call it premarital jitters or what, but

I just didn't want to make that kind of commitment when I wasn't one hundred percent sure," Mister stated.

"Then why would you ask me to marry you when you weren't sure? You don't know how bad you hurt me. Although I respect you for following what felt right to you, how do I know that you won't just back out again? I don't think I can handle that," I said.

"Just give me another chance. We have so much history together. I'm not going to lie, I've tried seeing other women but I want you. I've even been seeing a counselor. You know the reverend who was supposed to marry us, Reverend Turner? I've been seeing him for the past two months. We've been discussing why I felt a need to run away and lose everything that we've built. I wanna do whatever needs to be done to be with you and to make you happy," Mister stated sincerely.

"Why now? When we were living together, it was a hassle just for us to get engaged. I think sometimes that you only wanted to get engaged because you didn't want me to leave you and that was the only way for you to buy time to hold on to me," I said, becoming angry.

"That was a long time ago. I know it's going to take much more than a conversation and some roses to prove to you that I was another person, an immature guy who didn't know what he really wanted. I'm a man now and I want you. I know that I still have a lot of growing to do, but I want to grow with you. Together I think we can do this. It's not going to be easy, but I need for you to trust me, " Mister asked.

"I don't know. This is all so sudden. I just don't know what I want right now or what's right for me. I just got this promotion and to be honest, I don't think I have the strength to deal with you and that right now," I tiredly responded.

"Understandable. Just let me show what I have to offer. I want us to both talk to Reverend Turner. Once we're both on the same page, you're not going to know what hit you. I plan on us getting back to the way things used to be. Just watch," he said, as he grabbed me around my waist and pulled me closer.

"We'll see, we'll see," I said drifting slowly off to sleep.

PART II

9/TAYLOR

People often say, when it rains it pours. After the wonderful weekend Delaney and I had, we returned home on Sunday morning. Now you know I'm usually up in church each and every Sunday, but after the weekend I had and the troubles I've been going through with my mom, church was the last place I felt like being. I know, I know, when you're going through a storm, that's the first place you need to run, but I just wasn't up to it. Call me a huge sinner, but like I said, I wasn't up for it.

Delaney and I woke up early Sunday morning and drove back from Cape May to my house and I cooked him breakfast. After his performance the night before, brother man deserved a Golden Globe, Grammy, something. I was definitely planning on keeping this one and making him a winner.

After breakfast, which consisted of pancakes, turkey bacon, and eggs, we lounged around for a while and then he finally had to head on home. I was so happy because he really came through for me in my time of need. We talked and laughed and he held me close to let me know that he was there for me. He made sure I was good to go. I told you the brother was on point. He went on home and we spoke on the phone that evening. Mind you, I still hadn't heard from my mom. That was really worrying me.

Monday morning, I went on to work and it was business as usual. Now I told you how my supervisor irritates the hell out of me. She got on my nerves so bad that I snapped on her ass once and for all.

"Taylor, I was looking at your sign-in register and noticed

Only Fools Gamble Twice

you signed in for eight A.M. and I know for a fact that you didn't come in until 8:04. I want a leave slip for fifteen minutes," Celine said, placing her hands on her wide hips.

"Excuse me? Look, Celine, I don't have time for this. It's Monday and you're not going to start in on me today. I got in at 8:04 and I'll make sure not to leave until 5:05, okay?" I stated as calmly as a person could.

"No, you'll give me leave slip for fifteen. I leave early today and I won't be able to tell if you left at 5:05 or not. I want a leave slip!" she demanded.

"You know what? I'm going to speak to Abby. I'm requesting that I be moved to another department. I'm tired of this shit!" I exploded as I stood and stormed to the manager's office.

"You don't talk to me that way! I'm your supervisor." She followed, hot on my heels.

"Just leave me the hell alone. I'm warning you."

"Oh, so that's a threat!"

"Please, you're not worth my time."

"Oh, really, well maybe you need some time to cool off. You're suspended. Indefinitely!" she yelled as I turned the corner and walked down the hall to the general manager's office.

Of course by then, everyone in their cubicles was standing up, trying to see what the commotion was all about.

I stormed into Abby's office and she was on the phone. She waved me in and had a disturbed look on her face. "I see. I see. Well she's in here now. Let me talk to her and I'll call you if I need you to meet with us," Abby stated to I assume Celine.

Abby replaced the phone and stared at me for a moment, as if she were trying to decide how to handle the whole ordeal. "Well, Taylor. As you may have realized, that was Celine on the phone. There seems to have been a problem. Let me hear your side."

I explained to Abby exactly what had transpired and then requested that I be removed from Celine's department.

"I cannot allow that. You two are both an integral part of our team. You both are going to have to work a little harder to get along better."

"There is no getting along better with Celine. You don't know how many times I literally bite my tongue. She just doesn't know how to talk to people. She really needs some anger-management classes," I declared.

"Well, I realize that and I also realize you have a bit of a temper yourself. What can we do to make this a peaceful situation?"

"I don't know. I guess I can try a little harder. It's just been so tough on me lately," I began as I broke out in tears.

"Taylor, I don't know what is going on, but I think you need some time off. Why don't you take off this week? You're no good to yourself or anybody else for that matter. Go ahead, get out of here. Don't you think one time about this place," Abby stated compassionately.

After I thought about it, I had plenty of leave, since I hardly ever took off. I thanked Abby and went back to my desk, signed off from my computer, grabbed my belongings, and headed for the warm summer air that awaited me.

I called Delaney at work from my cell phone and got his

voice mail. I left a message for him, telling him that I was off for the rest of the week and to call me at home.

When I arrived home, I changed clothes and contemplated going for a run. Just as I was about to go upstairs and get prepared to go out for a run, my phone rang.

"Hey, sweetness. What's up? You don't feel good? Why are you at home?" Delaney questioned.

"I got into a little something with my supervisor and my manager suggested I take some much-needed time off."

"How long are you off?"

"For the rest of the week."

"I'm coming over to get you. Take a little vacation with me?"

"What? You just took me away for the weekend. We can't go back there again."

"Who said anything about going back there."

"Ah, excuse me, but don't you have to work?" I asked.

"I'm a consultant. As long as I configure a program for my company, I can come and go as I please. Besides, I told you I was going to see my mom."

"Yeah, but that was supposed to be in the next few weeks."

"Well, we can go this week. Nothing's stopping us. I'll just call my mom and tell her I'm coming two weeks early and I'm bringing my sweetness with me. C'mon. Go with me. It ain't like you got a job this week. What are you going to do, sit around and do nothing? Do nothing with me," Delaney stated excitedly.

"You don't think we're moving too fast? I mean after all,

we just met a few weeks ago and we both agreed to take things slowly. I feel like I'm in a tailspin."

"Yeah. We are moving fast, but then again, we're both adults. I'm not complaining. Are you?" he asked.

"Not at all. I'm having the time of my life, despite all that's happening. I'm just happy to have you here for me," I said.

"Well that settles it. We're going. Right?" he asked.

After careful thought, I figured it was a good idea. I didn't have any children and I could get my neighbor to feed my animal kingdom. Sure, I'd live on the wild side twice in my life, ride this wonderful escape for as long as chance would permit.

"Are you sure you want me to go with you?" I cautiously asked.

"I wouldn't have asked you if I didn't want you to go."

"When are we leaving and when are we coming back?"

"We can leave tonight and come back Saturday afternoon."

"Tonight? How are we going to get there?"

"I'm driving and now you can keep me company. Are you going to ask me a million questions or are you just going to go with me?"

"Alright. I'll go, but I have so many things to do and I have to pack and--."

"Well you just be ready by five-thirty. Drive over to my house and you can leave your car there. I'll see you later, sweetness."

I hit the Concord Mall with a vengeance. I bought so many clothes, enough to last a lifetime. I was so nervous, here I

Only Fools Gamble Twice

had just met this guy and already I was going off to another state to meet his family. I was pretty damn excited. I called Tyrone first to let him know of my plans and promised to call him the minute I arrived. I then called Morgan and got her voice mail, which stated she was away on a business trip. I had completely forgotten. I tried her cell phone and also got her voice mail, but I knew that she would check that. I left her a long message and told her of my plans. I knew she would be shocked as all hell, but would be totally happy that I had decided to go. Morgan always lives on the wild side.

  I arrived at Delaney's home after getting a manicure, pedicure, Brazilian wax, packing, and being utterly exhausted. He looked good as usual. I could have eaten him alive right there.

  We got on the road and made the long journey to Arkansas. When we arrived at Delaney's mom and stepfather's home early the next morning, we were both pretty tired. Although I was tired on the drive down, I refused to go to sleep and leave my baby up all by himself. I offered to drive several times, but he declined each and every time, said it relaxed him. So we listened to Travis Hunter's new book on tape, *Married But Still Looking*. The book was excellent and afterward we had a pretty intense debate about Genesis' character and if men could really change after being unfaithful. Once the book was completed, we talked about everything under the sun. He even asked me if he were the type of guy that I would marry. Of course I said, "Hell yeah."

  The week at Delaney's parents' home was probably the best time I'd had in quite a while. His mother, a slender dark-skinned woman in her mid-fifties, was quite the host. She fed me until I thought I would burst. At that rate I'd be hitting the gym until eternity. Of course she threw down on the cuisine and I didn't want to insult her by not eating her food. My grandmother, when she was alive, would cook the most awesome meals and would be seriously ready to cut you if you didn't eat until your eyes bulged out of their sockets.

    By the time Saturday rolled around, I was ready to go home. It was just a feeling of not sleeping in your own bed all week, too much food, and too much laughter.

    Delaney's stepfather is the family comedian and all week he told me these jokes that just weren't funny, but I laughed anyway. Delaney and I slept in the same room--his mother set it up that way. He tried desperately to get some nookie, but I wasn't having it. He kept saying his mother didn't care, but I did. I ain't disrespecting nobody's mama or her house. I kept checking my messages at home but my mother still hadn't called. I called my brother to ask if he had talked to her but he said that when he called my mother cursed him out and said not to ever call her again. I cried for a few minutes, then I dusted myself off and vowed not to shed one more tear about a situation I had no control over. I simply realized how blessed I was that I had someone who was there for me.

    Early Saturday morning rolled around and Delaney and I said our good-byes to the family. I truly thanked them for the wonderful time that I had and welcomed them to my home if they were ever in Delaware. Delaney's mom gave me a kiss and a peach cobbler for me to take home. I figured I would keep it on ice once we arrived home because I had also promised myself that I was never going to eat another piece of pie ever again.

Only Fools Gamble Twice

Once we were on the road and were pretty comfortable, I looked over and noticed how content my baby looked.

"You know my family really likes you," Delaney stated.

"Yeah, your family was really sweet to me. Now I see where you get it."

"Oh, so you think I'm sweet to you?"

"Yeah, you are sweet to me. This was the second time that I really needed to be swept away and you were there for me both times. I really appreciate it, and I just want to thank you."

"You don't need to thank me. It's been my pleasure."

"Well I do need to thank you. I don't know what I would have done if you hadn't been there for me. I'd probably be stuck in some looney bin by now."

"I'm just happy to be here for you. I wanna take good care of you. You're my sweetness," he said with a smile as he placed his hand over mine and gave it a tight squeeze.

I didn't tell Delaney, but I was really depressed. When I checked my voice mail before we got on the road, my brother Tyrone had left another message. Apparently Winston, my mother's asshole ex-husband, had gotten himself locked up and my mom called Tyrone to borrow the money to bail Winston out. Now mind you she told him to never call her again but then she turns right around and asks him for money. Tyrone used his rent money to loan to my mother but when he asked her to give it back she told him to go to hell. Now Ty wanted me to repay him. My brother suggested to my mom that she call me and she told my brother that she would never be speaking to me again. He said she was pretty angry when he even mentioned my name. I really couldn't understand why Ty continued to bother with her, now I had to fork over five hundred dollars for a problem that wasn't even mine.

"What's on your mind? You got all quiet on me all of a sudden," Delaney said, as we continued on our journey home.

"Nothing," I lied.

"Something's on your mind. You went from displaying that pretty smile to looking like you have the weight of the world on your shoulders."

"I'm just thinking about my mom."

"I've been thinking too. I know it's none of my business, but I think you should reach out to your pastor and let him know what's going on."

"I thought of that, but my mom's a very private person and I know she'd just lash out at anyone who tried to tell her what to do," I explained.

"I just want you to feel better. I know you're hurting right now. That's why I want to just be there for you."

"We don't really have a big family so just to have someone in my corner means a lot to me right now."

I didn't say much else. I think Delaney knew that I just needed time to myself in my own skin without many distractions.

When we finally arrived back to Delaney's home late Saturday evening I realized that I was more exhausted than I had thought. Again, I hadn't slept while he drove. There was a red Range Rover in the driveway.

"Shit."

"What's wrong?"

"Naw, that's Nina's Rover in the driveway."

"Who's Nina?" I asked calmly, thinking this was where

the happy ending turned ugly.

"Nina's my roommate's fiancée. I don't see his car, so that means he must be working. I don't see why she can't stay her ass at home when he's not here. She and I don't see eye to eye," he explained.

I calmed back down. No scene here. My ending had a chance to be happy after all. When we walked in, there was a tall, slim, light-skin woman laying on the couch with her legs draped over the side talking on the phone. She never budged, just looked at us like we were disturbing her and then rolled her eyes at Delaney and stared at me. She gave me a fake-ass smile. I couldn't quite figure her out so I decided to give her a fake-ass smile in return.

We went upstairs to place his bags down and Delaney pleaded with me to stay with him that night, and I couldn't think of a reason why I shouldn't, so I stayed. Plus, I was really enjoying his company and I just didn't want it to end just yet.

I had it all figured out. Delaney and I had talked about my career and I was going to call in tomorrow and demand a meeting with my manager, Abby. I wanted to do consulting work. I definitely had the skills and I knew that any company would be more than happy to hire me without a problem. I had already received several offers, but I wanted the job security. I decided it was time to work for me. I was too tired of punching a damn time clock and couldn't see myself doing that for the rest of my life.

We showered together in Delaney's room, which was a treat in itself. The man had it going on. I think we may have gotten a little too excited, because we then heard doors slamming. Of which we paid no mind. I could tell his roommate's fiancée was going to be trouble, just by the way she looked at me.

We slept until late Sunday afternoon. Sunday evening, we stayed in his room and ordered a pizza for dinner. Around 10:00 P.M. we were laying in the bed watching TV and Delaney asked if I wanted some ice cream. Since I had eaten like a pig all week, I declined, but asked for a glass of water instead. Delaney gave me a kiss on the forehead and told me he would be right back. After a few minutes, I heard loud voices downstairs. *What the hell is going on?* I thought. I then heard a door slam and then Delaney came in the room with a look on his face that made me scared. He slammed the door.

"I can't stand that slimy hoe!" he hollered. "She makes me the fuck sick!"

I didn't know what to do, so I just put the TV on mute and sat up in the bed. Finally he walked over to the bed and plopped down beside me.

"What's wrong, babe? Is everything all right?" I asked as I rubbed his back. He just turned around to look at me, then turned his head back around and put his face in his hands. I didn't say anything, I just continued to rub his back. After a few moments Delaney turned around.

"Do you know what my roommate's fiancée did?" he asked me with a look of disgust on his face.

"She had the nerve to walk up on me when I was in the kitchen and started rubbing all up against me. For a minute, I thought it was you, but then noticed something wasn't the same. I turned around and here's this hoe, all up in my face. Then she jumps her stankin' ass on the counter and starts playing with herself all up in my face. Talking about how my boy ain't doing his job and how she knows that I'm the man for to do what needs to be done. Do you believe that shit?" he asked me as he looked in disbelief.

"One of my other boys told me the hoe was slimy, but damn. Braxton is out here working hard for her ass and this is how she's acting. When he told me she would be staying here some nights while he worked the night shift, I knew it was a reason why I didn't want her here. Bitch thinks because she has those damn devil eyes and that light-ass skin, men are supposed to trip to get that beat up-ass," he continued.

I was amazed at the language coming from Delaney's mouth. I knew that even when I get upset there was no telling what I would say, but it was no stopping him.

"What makes it so bad is that she knows that you're up here. That's just downright disrespectful. I mean if you weren't here, I guess that hoe really thinks I would do her. Women come a dime a dozen. I'm supposed to do my boy's fiancé and not have no respect for him. We don't roll like that. What cracks me up is that this ain't the first time she tried this shit. Enough is enough, either that hoe goes, or I go. I'm just gon' have to lay down the law to my boy and let him know that his bitch is slimy.

"'Nough said." He stood and started to pace. I sat there in shock. What could I say? I was ready to go down there and get North Philly style on her ass, but I wasn't sure if that was the right move to make. I know that I didn't like to see him so upset. As Delaney continued to pace, I decided to go downstairs to get that glass of water that he never did bring to me. When I walked in the kitchen Nina was standing at the sink, with her back to me.

"You're pretty. What's your name, honey?" Nina asked as I went to the cabinet to get a glass.

"Well it damn sure ain't honey. I only let Delaney call me names like that," I replied, hoping this chick would push my button. I was looking to kick somebody's ass and let off some more steam.

"You must be from Philly with that attitude."

"As a matter of fact I am. You got any Vaseline?" I asked, hoping that Nina would get the hint that I was about to use it to bust her up.

"And a sense of humor too."

"I'm glad you think so," I replied.

"Did your man tell you that he tried to push up on me?" Nina asked as she jumped up on the kitchen counter, her long legs dangling.

"Push up on you? That's not quite the way I heard it," I said, with a light laugh.

"Oh, well, you know how men can change up a story to suit their needs. What do you even know about him?" Nina asked as she peered at me with her hazel-colored eyes.

Nina was a very attractive woman, but I could tell that she was accustomed to getting things her way, and did so by using her good looks. I knew that much. I see her type all the time. Now, yeah, I'm a good-looking woman myself, but I don't look so good that I don't know how to throw down and kick somebody's ass. Sista-girl was pushing ghetto girl outta me, and fast! I've worked long and hard to suppress her, but Miss Nina was looking for an ass whooping.

"First of all you don't know me from Adam. I've had a very long week and I suggest you bark up another tree. Go on now before you get told," I warned.

"Oh, I see, you're one of those gangsta girls," she replied.

"Well I'm gonna let you tell it. Now I warned you the first time. Don't make me open up a few cases of whoop ass on you," I warned again.

"I know that Delaney cares more about his boy than he cares about doing something like you. Seems like he has more respect for your man than you do," I said, pulling out the water pitcher and pouring my water.

"Look, you seem like a nice kid. You don't know what the hell you're talking about, only what he tells you. Everything was fine before you came. Now why don't you march your little ass back upstairs and mind your own business. Better yet, why don't you get the fuck out?" Nina shouted.

"Honey, don't catch a beat down up in here. This is my last time saying this, I had a long week and I'm not for it. I don't want to disrespect somebody else's house, but I will bust your ass. Don't play me close," I said as I put the glass down in the sink, just waiting for Nina's next move.

I heard Delaney's loud footsteps coming down the stairs.

"I know you ain't talking to her like that. I don't hit women, but I'll knock you on your ass. Now say something else. I'll--," Delaney began as Braxton walked in the front door.

"What the hell is going on? I heard you all screaming from outside. Yo Dee, man, why you all in my girl's face like that? That shit ain't cool, yo," Braxton said as he pushed his way in the kitchen, almost knocking me down, as he stood toe to toe in Delaney's face.

"Why don't you ask your bitch!" Delaney exploded.

"Yo, Dee man, don't be standing here disrespecting my woman. I done told you, man, that shit ain't cool. You my boy and everything but I'm gon' have to knock you the fuck out if you keep disrespectin' her," Braxton said, taking a step closer to Delaney.

"Come on, babe. He ain't worth it. It was just a big misunderstanding, that's all," Nina said, grabbing Braxton's arm and pulling him back.

"What the fuck is going on, babe? I ain't about no stupid shit. Will somebody tell me what the hell is going on?" Braxton said as he looked at Nina and then Delaney, not even seeing me.

"You ask Nina, when you get a chance, man. You and me gon' have to holler at each other. It's some foul shit goin' on here, man, and either I go or she goes. Come on, sweetness. Let's bounce," Delaney said as he turned to me, and led me upstairs.

When we got to Delaney's room, he sat on the bed and held his head down, rubbing it.

"How the fuck am I gon' tell my boy this shit. Sweetness, I don't want to stay here tonight. Can we go back to your place?" he asked as he looked up at me.

"Sure, sweetie, let's roll," I said as I turned to gather my belongings.

"Wait, I'm sorry you had to witness all that. It's not like you don't have enough drama going on in your life already. Man, the devil be working overtime to bring a brother down, doesn't he?" he said, shaking his bald head in disbelief.

"I'll rap to my boy tomorrow after work or something. By that time, everyone will have cooled down. Yeah, that's what I'm gon' do," Delaney said, more to himself than me. Just as I lifted the T-shirt over my head I heard a loud boom.

"What the hell," I said, as I yanked the T-shirt back down. Braxton had kicked the door in and had a look of rage on his face.

"You no-good motherfucker. How the hell you gon' try me like that!" Braxton said as he charged toward Delaney. Before Delaney had a chance to get up, Braxton caught Delaney in his left eye with a powerful punch. Delaney came up with an upper-cut to Braxton's abdomen and followed with a two piece to the grill. That two piece threw Braxton off balance.

I started screaming, "Stop it. Stop it," to no avail. I ran to get out of the way and to call 911. Delaney continued to throw three more punches, and the fourth knocked Braxton on the floor, unconscious. Suddenly, Nina came in the room all wild and crazy like something you would see on a bad made-for-TV movie. Anyway, while she was auditioning for her role in the next scary movie, I clocked the chick square in her jaw. She stumbled a bit and then I followed up with another jab to her chinny chin.

"Come on, let's bounce," Delaney said as he grabbed our bags. We headed downstairs when we heard a loud thump at the door.

"That's probably the police," I said as Delaney swung the door open.

"Sir, we got a disturbance call," the male officer said as his female partner looked past him to get a good look at me.

"Ma'am, are you all right?" the female officer asked.

"Oh, yes, officer, I'm okay," I answered, my nerves making me shake from the whole ordeal.

"My roommate and his girlfriend came upstairs and started fighting with us. You two can come in," Delaney said, stepping aside to allow the officers to enter.

"I'm Officer Romanowski and this is my partner Officer Caraway," the male officer stated.

"Where is your roommate and the other party now?" Officer Caraway asked as she looked around the house.

"They're both upstairs now, last door on your left," Delaney explained.

"Exactly what happened here?" Officer Caraway asked.

"My roommate burst down my door and charged toward me. We fought, and I think I knocked him out cold," Delaney said, as he rubbing his head.

"Did you call for an ambulance, sir?" Officer Caraway asked.

"I don't know," Delaney replied.

"I'll go. Caraway, get statements from these two while I make sure the roommate is okay," Officer Romanowski said as he headed up the stairs.

"Sir, is there anyone else in the house?" Officer Romanowski asked as he paused on the stairs.

"No, just the two of them," Delaney said, sitting down on the couch. Officer Caraway took our statements.

"Caraway, make a call on the radio, tell them we need to get an ambulance over here. I think this kid has a concussion," Officer Romanowski said.

Officer Caraway made the call for the ambulance. Then kept on grilling us about what happened. When the ambulance arrived, the EMTs were directed upstairs to get Braxton. When the EMT returned a few minutes later without Braxton, the puzzled looks on each of our faces made the EMT shrug.

"He's all right. He'll be fine. He'll just have a heck of a headache tomorrow. He doesn't need to go to the hospital," the EMT said as he and his partner headed for the door.

Officer Romanowski came down a few minutes later and asked Delaney if he could see him in the kitchen. From where I was sitting I could tell that whatever the officer was saying to him Delaney didn't like it. The officer called his partner to the kitchen and the three of them continued talking. After a few minutes Officer Romanowski and Delaney went upstairs and Officer Caraway returned to the living room.

"What's going on now?" I whispered.

"The roommate wants him out. It's his house and since they don't have an official lease, he has to vacate the premises. Your boyfriend was saying that he really doesn't have a place to stay. Said he's not from here and that his family is down South. It's unfortunate when these things happen," Officer Caraway said as she finished the police report.

Officer Romanowski and Delaney came back downstairs with several of Delaney's bags. Officer Romanowski helped Delaney place the bags into his Jeep. Officer Romanowski then gave Delaney one of his business cards and told him to call down to the station when he was ready to pick up his remaining belongings. Delaney came over to where I was sitting and grabbed my hand, leading me to the kitchen.

"Taylor, I hate to ask you this, but--" he began before I cut him off.

"Officer Caraway already told me what happened and I know your situation. I'm asking you to stay with me until you get on your feet. I trust you and I know that you've got my back. Now it's my turn to return all of the favors. I just hope my misfortune is not rubbing off on you. Besides, I need a good bodyguard and you're pretty good with that left hook," I said, looking up at him, giving him a smile that said I understood.

"I think I'm starting to fall hard for you," he said as he kissed me on the forehead and led me by the hand to the living room as we prepared to leave.

We thanked and apologized to Officers Romanowski and Caraway and they waited until we were ready to leave and then they made sure we were in our cars and had pulled off before they left the house.

Since Delaney did consulting he again decided that he didn't want to go to work so he used my computer and worked from home. Seeing him stay at home gave me even more inspiration. The time had come to make the move to start my own business.

I arrived to work at 7:00 a.m. I knew that Abby would be in since it seemed as if she practically lived in the office. I marched into Abby's office and notified her that I would be giving her my two weeks notice. I was hereby going to consult my services for a living. Now was as good a time as any. The old Taylor was back with a vengeance. The one that thought of herself first and foremost. The rest of the world would just have to sit back and watch my moves. It was all about me now.

10/MORGAN

My trip to New York was just what the doctor ordered. Speaking of which, I met this fine doctor while I was there. I had seen him a few times in the past when I attended a few pharmaceutical seminars. We always gave each other that knowing look, but it never went beyond a casual nod.

I arrived Sunday evening and while in the hotel restaurant, with one of my colleagues, Karen, I noticed him, the very attractive, dark brown brother with the smooth-looking skin, giving me the once-over. I tried to ignore him, but he just wouldn't quit. He then sent a bottle of Merlot over to our table and I knew that I needed to thank him for his generosity. I told the waiter to thank him and the doctor took that as an invitation to approach our table. I told my girl Karen what was going on and we agreed that she would stay if he turned out to be a weirdo and leave if he was cool. After about thirty minutes of laughter and me constantly eyeing Karen, trying to get her to take her ass back to her room or at least leave me the hell alone, I finally stepped on her foot and that gave her the final signal that her services were no longer needed.

Karen's a cool Asian girl I met several years ago and we always seemed to end up on the same business trips sponsored by Remy Pharmaceuticals.

The doctor's name was Collin. He was a client of one of our competitors. He was the funniest man I'd ever met. He was really down to earth and his warm personality made me feel like I'd known him for an eternity. We really hit it off, almost instantly.

Collin invited me to go out to a club with him and a few others who were staying at the hotel for the same convention that we were attending. Not one to turn down a chance to party, I accepted.

Collin was originally from New Orleans, but currently lived in Upstate New York. All of my friends who reside in New York are nothing but party animals, and Collin proved to be down with the set. My one night of hanging out with him and the other brothas and sistas at the convention, proved to be the time of my life.

We must have partied all week and by Thursday, I wanted a vacation from my convention. I could barely keep my eyes open during our workshops. Now don't hate me when I tell you this, but Thursday evening, we all went out again and the club we were at wasn't quite jumping for a Thursday night. We decided to call it an early night, which was all of midnight. When we arrived back to the hotel we saw Al from the Atlanta office and Theresa from the Houston office. Who were heading out for a night on the town.

"Hey, where are you two heading?" I asked.

"Girl, we're going to the Copa, this after-hour spot. You two should come with us."

It took all of a look and Collin and I were turning back around heading out for a second time out on the town that night, or rather that morning.

We arrived and the place was jam-packed. It was salsa night and I was really feeling that meringue. There was another side to the club and they were playing hip-hop and R&B. Collin, who is just as much a party animal as me, was by my side the entire time, nonstop.

Only Fools Gamble Twice

    I don't remember if it was Al or Collin, but I know that someone pulled out cigars and each of us took puffs. I knew that I had way too much to drink, but since I wasn't driving, no harm, no foul.

    Around three o'clock I knew that I had enough and was ready to head back to the hotel. Although we only had a few things to go over in our seminar, I still had to get up early and pack.

    "Hey, Collin, I'm about to bounce," I stated loudly in his ear.

    "Why? The party is just getting started. This is our last night together. I don't want it to end. I've really enjoyed myself with you over the last few nights. You're cool peeps."

    I decided to stay a little while longer, but after about a half hour I thought my feet were actually bleeding. Luckily, Collin, Al, and Theresa were ready to bounce too.

    Theresa suggested we go to an all-night diner and so that's what we did. Me, practically crawling to the taxi, because you couldn't tell me my feet were not broken from all that damn dancing. I mean, I can party with the best of them, but Collin actually wore me out.

    Breakfast was absolutely delicious. I don't know if it was because I was starving, tired, hung over or what. I just practically swallowed my food and got a terrible case of Negroitis afterward. I just wanted to sleep.

    Friday morning rolled around way too soon and I didn't know how I was ever going to make it out of bed and down to my seminar. Somehow, I mustered enough energy to get up, shower, and arrive to my final workshop on time. By the end of the workshop I said my good-byes to all of my newfound friends, and Collin and I vowed to stay in touch. He wanted me to actually come up and see him in New York, real soon, and I was definitely going to take a little trip to see him.

He tried to push up on me a few times. The brother had it going on, but I had enough things on my plate at the time.

Before I left the hotel I tried phoning Kofie so I could possibly catch lunch with him before I headed back on the train. I received his voice-mail and I even beeped him. After a few minutes a woman returned my call.

"Did someone beep this number?"

"Yes, I was looking for Kofie," I replied, becoming suspicious.

"Who's calling?" the woman asked with a hint of attitude.

"With whom am I speaking?"

"This is his wife," she stated.

"Really now?" I said, becoming angry.

"Really. Now do you mind telling me who you are?"

"Yeah, I do. If you're his wife then I guess I really don't need to speak with him, now do I? You have a good day," I said as I released the button in her ear.

I wasn't remotely angry with sista-girl but I definitely didn't appreciate Kofie's lying. I was way too exhausted to deal with the drama at the moment. I had a train to catch and sleep to get.

When I arrived home Friday evening, I wanted nothing more than to just grab a glass of wine and relax, with no interruptions from anybody. I turned off the phone, turned on my Jaguar Wright CD, and chilled. I didn't even check for messages. They'd still be there the next day.

That night, I probably slept better than I had in years. I awakened the next morning to a rainy day. Perfect for just being lazy. I made some coffee and toast and decided to pop in one of my workout tapes. I finally checked all of my messages from the week and realized I had almost ten from Mister. He wanted to know why I hadn't called him while I was away. Kofie called and wanted to know why I hadn't called him either. *Excuse me?* I had to check to see when that message had come in. I checked and sho 'nuff brother man had actually called the night before. So he must not have gotten word from his wife that I had called. Whatever!

I had a call from my father. I thought that was strange because my dad practically never called my house. He usually waited for me to call or would just tell my mother what he wanted and I'd then speak with him. I guess men and phones would never be the best of friends.

I immediately dialed my parents' home. It took three rings before a woman answered.

"Hello, this is Morgan. Who is this?" I asked the woman.

"Oh, so now you don't know my voice. It's your sister, stupid. Where have you been? We've been looking all over for you," my older sister, Jewel, responded. All of a sudden I got a gut-wrenching feeling in the pit of my stomach. Jewel and her husband lived in Dallas, and for her to be there without telling me she was coming was odd. I instantly thought something was wrong. Was her marriage on the rocks?

"Mom's in the hospital," Jewel said, interrupting my thoughts.

"Hospital? What do you mean? I just talked to her," I said before my voice trailed off. I had been so busy with my convention and work that I hadn't talked to my mother since I had left for New York. Normally we talked about twice a week, but there was no excuse for me not to call her more often.

"Dad rushed her to the hospital late last night. He called you from the hospital, but he got your voice mail," Jewel said. interrupting my thoughts.

"For what?" I exploded.

"Calm down. The doctors are running tests. We don't know yet. They're still running tests. Where were you? We tried reaching you all last night."

"I was in New York at a convention for work all week. I just got home last night. Mom knew that I was going, but I never left her the number where I was staying. I had my cell phone and figured if she needed me she would call me on that. Why didn't dad call me on my cell phone?"

"He probably doesn't even know the number. You know Daddy."

"What hospital is Mom in?" I asked, changing the subject abruptly.

"Christiana Hospital. Harold and I flew in early this morning. Dad called us last night and we didn't waste anytime getting here. We're on our way to the hospital now. Dad hasn't been home since then," Jewel stated.

"The doctors don't have any idea what's wrong with Mom?"

"Why don't you get over to the hospital. Like I said,

they're still running tests right now," Jewel whispered into the receiver.

Call me crazy, but I just didn't buy my sister's story. You don't get rushed to the hospital in the middle of the night to get a bunch of tests.

"What's going on, Jewel? Tell me what the hell is going on?" I demanded.

"It's cancer. Mom's in surgery right now. Let's pray everything will be alright. I didn't want to worry you over the phone."

"Worry me? I have a right to know about my own damn mother. You can't just lie to me. What did you think, I wasn't going to find out!" I screamed into the receiver.

"Calm down. We need to keep it together for Mom right now," my sister insisted. "Apparently Mom and Dad have known for some time that Mom was sick, but they didn't want to worry us," Jewel said, as her voice began to crack.

"I'm on my way to the hospital. I'll see you there," I said before I hung up the phone.

"I know you're not into church or anything, but say a prayer for Mom, I think she's going to need it," Jewel said before we hung up the phone.

Jewel and Harold were supposedly born-again Christians and pretty much spent all of their free time in the church. Ain't nothing like a lying Christian. Jewel sat right there and lied about the severity of my mother's condition but yet she's going to question if I say prayers. Later for that argument. I said a quick, silent prayer, then ran upstairs to change into a pair of jeans.

While I was getting changed, the phone rang again. I

thought of not answering but rethought that idea, not knowing if it was Jewel calling.

"Hello, pretty lady," Kofie said softly in the phone.

"What do you want?" I stated in an agitated tone.

"It's me, Kofie."

"I know damn well who it is. What do you want?"

"Why do you speak to me in such a manner?"

"Why don't you ask your wife?"

"I do not have a wife. I explained that to you already."

"Look, Kofie, I really don't have time right now to deal with this," I said as I replaced the receiver.

Almost instantly the phone rang again, "Look damn it, I said I don't have time for this shit," I yelled.

"Well hello to you too. What's wrong? You sound upset?"

"What the hell do you want? I gotta go!' I barked into the receiver, as tears slowly welled up in my eyes.

"Wait. What's wrong?"

"My mom's in the hospital and I gotta get over to there right now. I gotta go."

"What hospital is she in? I can drive you. You're in no condition to be driving. Wait there, I'll be there. I'll be there in five minutes," Mister stated. He hung up in my ear before I could object.

Mister arrived in record time, about three minutes. He lived practically a few blocks from my home, so I knew that he'd be there in no time. Besides, for some reason I just didn't want to go to that hospital alone. As strong as everyone says that I am, I suddenly felt so weak.

When Mister and I arrived at the hospital, my dad, sister,

and brother-in-law were all in the waiting room.

"Hey, Daddy. I'm so sorry. I was in New York all week. I just got home. How's Mom?" I asked as I gave my dad a hug.

"Don't worry about it, sweetheart. All that matters is that you're here now. They have your mother in surgery now. They're trying to see if they can stop the cancer from spreading. The doctor came out before you arrived. She said we should know something soon," my father said.

"Daddy, why didn't you two tell us what was up?"

"Your mother didn't want to worry either of you. We wanted to wait until we knew more about this whole thing," Daddy explained.

I started to argue my point to my daddy, but felt that wasn't such a good idea. Being such a strong and dominant figure, I hadn't seen my father worry too often, but this time he looked tired and scared. I sat and waited with my family with Mister by my side to hear what the doctors had to say. Mister placed his hand on mine and I suddenly realized how much of an asshole I had been to him.

"I apologize for the way that I spoke to you earlier. I had a lot on my mind and I shouldn't have taken it out on you," I explained.

"It's all good. I'm just glad I called when I did. I want to be here for you."

"Well, thanks," I replied.

About an hour later the doctor told us that my mother was out of surgery and that for now everything looked good.

"We want to keep her under observation for the next forty-eight hours. After that, we'll know where we stand. For now, however, all looks well. It'll be a while before you can go in to see her but she'll need plenty of rest. If she continues to stabilize we'll allow her to go home in a few days but we'll need to begin aggressively with chemotherapy treatment," the young doctor explained.

We each felt the tension was lifted, and Harold led all us in a brief prayer, thanking God for pulling my mother through with no problems. We asked the Lord for a speedy recovery for my mom and that the cancer would be defeated. The doctor said we could see my mom for a few minutes, but then we would have to let her rest.

After another hour of waiting we were finally able to visit with her. When we walked in the room, she was laying in her bed asleep. I thought that even under these circumstances my mother still looked good, actually she looked like she was at peace with no pain. "Hey, baby, I found all of these kids in the hallway looking for you," my daddy whispered as he gently placed a light kiss on my mother's forehead.

My mother opened her eyes and began smiling.

"How you feeling, Mom?" Jewel asked.

"Like I just came out of surgery," Mom said, making us all laugh.

"Jewel, how is she supposed to feel? Don't pay her any attention, Mom," I said, stepping closer to my mother, giving her a wet kiss on the cheek. "I want you to get better so we can get you home and take good care of you," I stated.

Mom patted my hand. It was hard for her to speak with all of the tubes they had her hooked up to.

As we were wrapping up the reunion session, the nurse came into the room and requested we leave so my mother could get her rest. Of course we protested but in the end, my mother even told us that she was extremely exhausted and needed us to head on home.

After staying at the hospital all afternoon, we were all exhausted. My dad decided to stay at the hospital but wanted us to go home. He promised us he wouldn't stay all night. We knew he was lying, but who could argue with a man who had been happily married to the same woman for thirty-three years? He wasn't about to go anywhere until he made sure Mom was okay.

Mister took me home and I realized that I still didn't want to be alone. I invited him to stay for dinner and we decided to order a pizza and rent a DVD. No matter how hard I tried, I just couldn't get back to my normal self because I knew that my mother was sick. Until she fully recovered and was home, I wouldn't be the same. Mister tried to cheer me up, but I just didn't feel like being bothered.

"I know you're depressed, baby. But don't worry, your mom is going to be fine. Here, drink this, it'll relax you and get your mind off of your worries," Mister said as he brought me a glass of vodka and orange juice.

I don't normally drink hard liquor. I just keep it in the cabinet for my friends when they come over, but after the day I had, I needed to take the edge off. After a few sips of the drink, I felt a little better and I allowed myself to relax for the first time that day.   Mister stayed with me that night and actually slept in the guest bedroom. I thought it was sweet of him to stay and not even try to resort to his old Mister ways. The following morning, I awakened earlier than normal. I called the hospital and spoke with my dad. He said Mom was looking a little better and they had removed most of the tubes. They were waiting for the doctor to arrive to see if Mom would be able to go home soon. After my call with my dad I felt restless so I called Taylor because I knew she would be up getting ready for church.

"Hey, girl, what's up!" I stated.

"You sound horrible. Everything okay?"

"Girl, I've had the worse day of my life. I got back from New York last night only to learn that my mom was admitted into the hospital," I explained.

"What! Oh my God, is she going to be alright?"

"She has cancer--"

"What?" Taylor interrupted.

"Yeah, she had an operation yesterday but they're keeping her for observation now. We saw her yesterday and she appeared to be doing fine but you never know with these things. Just pray for her, Taylor."

"Oh, no doubt," Taylor stated.

We spoke for a few more minutes and then I had to run. Taylor told me that we really needed to talk, but that she was busy, so we made plans to meet later on in the week so she could fill me in on the drama in her life. It felt that life had changed so much in the last two weeks. Almost like an eternity.

When I got off the phone with Taylor, I realized how hungry I was. I decided to fix a big breakfast for Mister and me. That was the least I could do. I looked in the refrigerator, but the only thing in there was bagels, bacon, and eggs. I knew that Mister really liked my home fries, but since I didn't have any potatoes, he would just have to eat what I had. As I began breakfast, the phone rang. *Who could be calling me this early in the morning?* I thought.

"Hello," I said dryly into the receiver.

"Good morning, sunshine. I hope I didn't wake you," Kofie said in his heavy accent.

"Why do you keep calling me? I have nothing to say to you. Please don't call me again," I warned.

"Please, please let me explain."

"There's no need to, you can save the drama for someone who really cares. All of you African men are all alike."

"Do not insult me in such a way!" Kofie stated, becoming angry.

"Oh, you don't think having me talk to your wife is insulting?"

"Is that what she told you? Did she also tell you we're getting a divorce? She came to the shop today to plead with me to stay with her. Let me explain it over dinner?"

"Kofie, I don't care to ever speak to you again."

"Look, is it that American boy?" I can make you so much happier. I'm going to Cameroon next week and I'll be gone for about a month. Let me see you before I go?" he asked.

"Do you hear yourself? Beat it. Get lost. I never want to talk to you again. You can just lose my number."

"Never. Don't play games with me. I want to be with you. I will call you when I return. Don't let a little situation with my wife stop us from really getting to know each other. I don't love her. It's simply a matter of convenience."

"I thought you were getting a divorce. You can't even keep your lies straight. I don't even know why I'm wasting my time talking to you," I said.

Before I could hang up the phone Mister came in the room. "Hey, babe? Whatcha got good to eat. I'm starving,"

Mister asked as he pressed up behind me. I wasn't quite sure how much of the conversation he heard, but knowing him I'm sure he at least heard part of it.

I shoved him away and gave him the dirtiest look, but he just turned away and walked over to the fridge. I was pissed as all hell. Every time I tried to give this asshole an inch he took a yard. "Who is that?" Kofie asked.

"*Excuse you?* That is absolutely none of your business."

"I don't like the way that you are speaking to me. Is that your boyfriend that you were telling me about? What can that American boy do for you? I would treat you like a queen," Kofie said.

"Oh, no you didn't?" I stated, completely at a loss for words.

"I'll call you back some other time when you're not playing games," Kofie replied and hung up.

I placed the handset back in its cradle and was totally pissed off. I couldn't believe what just happened.

"What's wrong, baby? What's for breakfast?"

"Why the hell did you do that?" I asked.

"Do what? I can't ask you what you have to eat?"

"You know damn well what you did. That's exactly why we can't get along now."

"We get along just fine. I'm sorry if you're upset with me. Now, let's go out to breakfast. I'm starving and I'm treating."

I was still mad, but I wasn't up for a bunch of arguing and I knew that there was no winning with Mister. Besides, I was hungry. Kofie, on the other hand was going to get cursed out beyond belief. I knew sooner or later his true colors would appear. But I just didn't have the strength to deal with that crap at the moment. I had a mother to get healthier.

Mister and I went to one of my favorite breakfast spots in New Castle and of course the food was great. Going out is always better when a) you don't have to cook and b) you don't have to pay for it.

After breakfast I realized that I had a few errands to run. After promising Mister I'd stop over after I took care of all of my business, I had him drop me back off at home. I changed clothes and then decided that I wanted to go up to the hospital to see my mom. When I arrived at her room, she was laying in bed with my father next to her. My sister and Harold were on their way to the hospital, and then they would be heading back to Dallas. Jewel and Harold didn't have any children and they both were lawyers for large firms in downtown Dallas, so they could afford to take a trip at a moment's notice, without being financially burdened. My Mom, Dad and I talked for a while.

Mom wanted to hear all of the details about my trip to New York. My dad excused himself and I told my mother about all the fun I had in the Big Apple. I told her about Collin and that I was probably going to travel back to New York to see him as soon as I knew she was back to normal.

"What about Mister? Are you two ever going to get back together?"

"Mom, I don't know. Right now, I'm just out having fun, living my life. He wants to get back together, but I don't know if I can trust him. You know Mister is full of surprises with his fair-weather self," I explained.

"Think about it. You two have history together. I know that Mister can be hard around the edges sometime, but it's rough finding a good man these days. I'm so happy I have your father. I wouldn't want to date in these days for all the tea in china."

When Jewel and Harold arrived at the hospital they stayed awhile, all of us talking like we were in my parents' family room. My father left with Jewel and Harold soon after to take them to the airport. I was relieved he hadn't asked me to take them because I wanted to have some private, quiet time with my mom. "So, tell me, Mom, should I really be concerned here? You are going to pull through this, right?" I asked with concern.

"I'm going to be fine. I'll be home before you know it. I ain't going nowhere, girl. I have a wonderful husband, two beautiful daughters, and a great son-in-law. Not to mention the stack of work piled to the ceiling on my desk. Besides, I have one daughter left to marry off. Then I have to get me some grandchildren before I leave this Earth. Do I sound like I'm going anywhere?" Mom said, looking for a moment like she was back to her normal self.

Mom and I continued to talk until my dad returned and then I started to feel like three was a crowd. I said good-bye and then told my mom that I would return the following day after work. It wasn't like I had to leave, but my parents always seemed so in love. They had a way of tuning out others around them, so if they were in a crowded room they couldn't even notice the other people. When they looked at each other, you could see the respect and love they had for each other. I always longed for the type of love my parents had, but realistically, does that kind of love exist today?

On my way home, I started to feel like my old self again. I

guess after seeing my mom feeling better after one day of recovery and us talking like we normally did, I allowed myself time to relax. When I arrived home, Mister had left a message for me to stop by for dinner. I looked into the fridge again and realized that I still had no food. I desperately needed to do some shopping, but as long as Mister had a free meal for me, I was grabbing it. I called him and told him I was on my way, and as I replaced the receiver, the phone rang. I thought it was Mister calling back to tell me to bring something.

"Hello, pretty lady. Are you able to talk *now*," Kofie's accent boomed though the phone.

"What do you want!" I asked in an irritated tone.

"Why are you speaking to me this way? I don't tolerate my women speaking to me in this manner."

"I cannot believe you are the same individual that I went out with last week," I stated.

"I could easily say the same thing. You tell me of this American boy who broke your heart and now you're back with him. What can this boy do for you?" Kofie asked.

"First of all, I don't deal with boys. Mister is a man. He may have issues like we all do, but do not ever question who I see or I don't. You don't know me well enough to do that!"

"Where is all of this attitude coming from. I am very offended. That's the problem with you American women. You don't know how to talk to a man. You all have very nasty attitudes."

"Well you know what? You don't have to be offended. Refrain from calling me anymore," I stated as I pushed the button in Kofie's ear.

After my call with Kofie, I felt like screaming. Here I

was dealing with this wanna-be king of Africa who was trying to check me. Ain't no way was I having that.

When I arrived at Mister's house, he had the place cleaner than the Board of Health and there were candles all throughout his living room and kitchen. Glenn Lewis' CD was playing in the background. I felt really comfortable and relaxed as soon as I walked into the room. I just hoped boyfriend didn't think he was back in after the other night when we were at the Butter Cup Lounge, since we had been spending some time together.

"What's all this?"

"It's a part of my surprise that I have for you."

"And what surprise would that be?" I asked with attitude. I just wasn't in the mood for his nonsense. I had a lot on my mind.

"Just be patient. I'll show you after dinner."

"Speaking of which, what's for dinner? It's smells good in here."

"Have a seat and relax. I'm almost finished. We can eat in a few minutes. I hope you're hungry."

"It feels like I haven't eaten in a year. I'm practically starving," I said as I had a seat and began to calm my nerves.

I concluded I may as well enjoy myself while Mister had gone through so much to prepare a nice meal for me.

"Good, I hope you like it," Mister said as he continued to stir something in a pot.

Mister prepared a meal that was simply delicious. We had a Caesar salad, chicken Parmesan topped with mushrooms served with a white wine and for dessert he made this banana-and-vanilla-ice cream-concoction covered with a caramel sauce. I thought I was going to explode from all that I had eaten, but everything was so amazingly good. I knew that Mister could cook, but this time he put his foot in it. After dinner, I helped him with the dishes and then he became all nervous.

"What are you up to?"

"It's the surprise I was telling you about."

"What is it?" I asked, beginning to become cautious.

"These," he said as he pulled out an envelope.

There were two round-trip tickets to Cancun.

"You're going to Cancun?" I asked.

"No silly, I want you to go to Cancun with me," Mister said, hopefully.

"Cancun? You and me?" I asked, stalling.

"Yeah, I know you've been under a lot of stress lately and I also know that I made the biggest mistake of my life walking out on our relationship. I want another chance to make this right. I love you."

"I don't know what to say. My mother is still in the hospital and I'm bombarded with work right now. Besides that, I need to be honest. I don't know about us."

"I'm sure your mom will be okay and you're allowed to take a vacation. Besides, don't you owe it to yourself to see if what we have can be salvaged? I realize now more than ever what you mean to me."

"I think you're being awfully selfish right now. I mean my mom just had surgery."

"How about this, why don't you talk it over with your parents and see what they say."

Everything was happening so fast. One minute I was completely in my own world and now all of this. I really didn't know what to do, but a trip to Cancun did sound quite inviting. What was a girl to do?

"Why didn't you ask me first?" I asked, not knowing what to say or do about this surprise trip.

"Uh, it's called a surprise," Mister replied sarcastically.

"And you're just so sure that I'd accept your invitation?"

"It's not that, I was hoping that you'd want to go with me. What do you say?"

"When is this trip taking place?"

"Next Friday we can leave for four days, three nights, we'll be staying at the Moon Palace. It's a five-star hotel. I'm sure you'll have a good time, if you'll just allow yourself."

"I think I will run it by my parents to see what they have to say first. There's no way that I can even imagine leaving the country without knowing my mom's status. I'll call her right now," I explained.

I called my dad on his cell phone and explained my dilemma. My dad told me that the doctors were releasing my mom in a few days and that I should go and take the time away to relax and not worry. He explained that Mom was in the best hands.

When I got off the phone I said, "I guess we're headed to sunny Cancun for a few nights but I'm still worried about my mom."

"I can understand that. May I make a suggestion?" Mister asked.

"Shoot."

"How about we enjoy the rest of the evening with each other and then we can go see your mom tomorrow and maybe the visit will put your mind at ease."

"Sounds like a plan," I agreed.

"You don't know how much I was worried that I had lost you. We're going to have a great time, you just wait and see," Mister said as he approached me with a warm hug.

On Monday morning, I arrived to work at 6:30. Henrietta arrived about ten minutes later. Together, as the work came in, we completed each project. Around ten, Bernie phoned me and asked to see me in his office. When I arrived, Bernie was standing at his secretary's desk. I said hello to Betty and then Bernie and I went into his office.

"Have a seat, Morgan. How are you this morning?" he asked.

"I'm good, and you?" I asked as I crossed my legs.

"I called you in because I wanted to give you a heads-up about the merger and where we stand with all that is going on. I want to ask that you to keep what I'm about to tell you, in the strictest of confidence. The takeover of Remny Pharmaceuticals will be occurring tomorrow, as far as we know. At that point we can relax a bit and the longer hours will not be required as much. I just wanted to let you know that I think that you're doing a remarkable job and after all of this is said and done, I'll be requesting that you are given an incentive award. As I said, keep this under wraps," Bernie said as he extended his hand and stood. "Good job. Keep up the good work."

"Thanks Bernie, I really appreciate it. It's nice to know that my work hasn't gone unnoticed," I said as I reached to shake Bernie's hand. He asked me how my weekend was, as he always did and I decided that I didn't want to reveal to him all that had occurred. I simply stated that I did much of nothing

Only Fools Gamble Twice

and a lot of everything. You know we all have those kinds of weekends. I also asked him for a week off for my trip, and of course he granted me the time off. Bernie then began walking me to the door and I followed him out of his office. Bernie, Betty, and I talked for a few moments and then I excused myself to get back to work. When I got back to my desk, Henrietta gave me a folder with new account information and then I went back into my cubicle. I retrieved my messages and was surprised that one of them was from Collin. I dialed his number and he answered on the second ring.

"Dr. Jenkins speaking," Collin stated in his deep baritone voice.

"Hey, Collin. It's Morgan," I said cheerfully.

"Well, well, well, if it's not Miss Lady. Why haven't I heard from you sooner?"

"How are you, Collin?" I responded, ignoring his question.

"I'd be doing better if you would have called me over the weekend."

"You could have called me, you know. Besides, I had a horrible weekend."

"What was so horrible about your weekend?"

"When I got home Friday, I just relaxed because you know you wore me out last week and I never checked my messages. Saturday, when I finally did check them, I had a message from my father that my mother was in the hospital. She has cancer," I explained, not really wanting to think about all of this, but Collin was a great listener.

"I'm so sorry to hear about that. I apologize for being such an ass. If there's anything I can do for you or if I can refer

Only Fools Gamble Twice

you to a specialist in the area, just let me know. What hospital is she in and what's her doctor's name?"

"She's in Christiana Hospital, her doctor's name is Nolan."

"I have a colleague over at the Fox Chase Cancer Center. His name is Alex Inman, he's the best. Give him a call and maybe he can tell you of some other options. I'll e-mail you with his phone number and his background information. I'm so sorry to hear about your mother, Morgan," Collin stated with utter concern.

"Thanks, Collin. I really appreciate that. Hopefully, when all of this over, I can make a visit to New York and we can hang out."

"Never mind about that. You just get your mother straight and we'll hang out soon enough. I'm going to e-mail you right now. I'll talk with you real soon. Take care and stay focused. Again, let me know if I can be of any assistance to you. I gotta watch my girl's back. You're good people."

"Thanks again, Collin. I really appreciate it."

"No problem. I'll talk with you soon."

True to his word, Collin e-mailed me the information and I decided to call the hospital to speak to my mom.

"Hey, good-looking."

"Hey, baby. I was just in here talking to the doctor. They're going to let me leave in a few days. I'll call you back in a little while."

"You sound good. How are you feeling?"

"I feel much better. I'll give you a call when we're done."

"Good, because a friend of mine just e-mailed me some

information about the Fox Chase Cancer Center. Call me when you're finished and we'll discuss it."

"Will do, baby," Mom replied.

I got off the phone, feeling much better. I was extremely relieved that my mom was doing better.

11/TAYLOR

It had been more than a week and Delaney and I were really getting along great as roommates. We each took turns cooking and cleaning and so far, no complaints over here. Although I had spoken to Tyrone, I still hadn't heard from my mother and I wanted to know how Malik was doing. So I decided that enough was enough, so I called.

"Yeah?" Winston barked into the receiver on the first ring, obviously with a chip on his shoulder.

I figured I would be the more mature person and not feed into his attitude.

"Hi, Winston, is my mother there?"

"Yeah?"

"May I speak with her?"

"Hold on." I could hear him in the background.

"Baby. Baby," he yelled.

"Who is it?" my mother yelled in the background.

"It's your daughter." Winston yelled back.

After a few minutes my mother got on the phone. "Yeah, what's up?"

"Hello to you too," I replied sarcastically.

"Don't call here starting your crap, Taylor. I ain't for it today."

"*Excuse me?*" I responded, now becoming not only angry, but hurt. How could my mother speak to me so harshly? What had gotten into her?

"You heard me. If you're calling to apologize than let's hear it."

"Mom, Winston should be the one apologizing. I don't think I've done anything wrong, but if that's what it's going to take to get this family back together again, than yes, I apologize," I stated warmly.

"What do you mean, Winston should be the one apologizing? Your brother and you have never liked Winston and you two will do anything to go against him. I want it to stop right now! I love him and he's not going anywhere."

"What about church and all you've worked hard to accomplish? Now you're drinking and goodness knows what else."

"You can just stop it right the fuck there! I'm the goddamn mother! You better not forget who the fuck it is that you're talking to. Now don't make me go there."

"Look at you, fussing and cussing. Using the Lord's name in vain. I don't know what's wrong with you."

"You and your brother are what's wrong with me. Y'all ain't happy unless I'm as miserable as the two of you. I've found happiness and I'm sorry if it doesn't come bottled up in some bourgeoisie ass way that you want it to come."

"You know, Mom, like you used to say to me, that is before you got all brainwashed and what not--and for the record, I'm going to pray for you--but like you used to say to me, 'only fools gamble twice. Remember that?"

"Fuck you, Taylor!" Mom said as she banged the phone in my ear.

That was it. I resolved myself to pray for my mom's deliverance. That's not to say that I don't need deliverance of my own. I mean Delaney and I had been doing things that are not of God's will, but I would pray for both my mother and me.

I hung up the phone and for some reason I wasn't feeling all that bad about my conversation with my mother. I was upset, don't get me wrong, but at the same time I realized that the situation was absolutely out of my control. From there on out all I could do was pray and be patient. God would have his way with us all, when He got ready. I did resolve, however, to make sure Malik was doing okay. If it meant going up to his school to talk to him then that's what I was planning to do. I was surely going to be there for him. It was my obligation to do so.

Delaney had gotten up early and gone to the gym. When he returned he came bursting through the door. "Hey, sweetness, I'm going over to Braxton's to get some of my things. You coming?" he asked as he pulled off his sweatpants and headed upstairs to the shower. I followed him.

"You think that's a good idea? That cop said to call him before you go over there."

"Then I'll call him and tell him to meet me over there. I'll feel a whole lot better when I have all my things out of there until I find another place to live," Delaney said as he picked up the phone.

Delaney asked for Officer Romanowski and after a few minutes the officer came to the phone. Delaney told the officer that he wanted to get his belongings and Officer Romanowski agreed to meet us there in thirty minutes.

When we arrived at Braxton's house, Nina answered the door.

"Yeah, what do you want?" Nina sneered as she stood with her hand on her hip.

"I want my..." Delaney began before Officer

Romanowski motioned for him to be quiet.

"Mr. Love is here to retrieve his belongings. I'm here to see that he gets those things and then he'll gladly leave," Officer Romanowski said politely to Nina.

"Whatever. But I don't think you're going to find much here. Whatever he didn't take, oh well," Nina said with a smirk.

"What? Don't let my stuff be..." Delaney began again before Officer Romanowski cut him off.

"Ma'am, we're not here for any trouble. If you'll just step aside, I'll escort Mr. Love upstairs to get his belongings," Officer Romanowski said, now becoming irritated by Nina's obvious attitude.

Delaney and Officer Romanowski made their way upstairs and Nina and I stayed downstairs. Nina just stared at me, looking me up and down. Finally I had enough. "What exactly is your problem? Are you some kind of lesbian or something? I don't do women," I said as I rolled my eyes.

"I don't normally do them either, but if the price is right I'll do you for a discount," Nina said as she licked her lips.

"You know you're one of those psycho hoes. You better stop playin' games. You're barking up the wrong damn tree today. Keep trying me and see if I don't bust you in ya damn mouth and give you a reason to lick those damn lips. Ass gon' be lickin' blood from that damn mouth in a minute," I said as I stepped in Nina's face. We heard a loud voice from upstairs and I knew that someone had gone way too far.

Just then Delaney came running down the stairs, Officer Romanowski on his heels. Delaney lunged for Nina, but the officer was quicker, pulling him back.

Only Fools Gamble Twice

"Come on now, Mr. Love. It's not worth it. You don't want to spend the night in jail. Handle this the right way," Officer Romanowski said as he tried to calm Delaney.

"Come on, baby. Whatever it is, it can't be that bad. Let's go. It's not worth, it like Officer Romanowski said," I responded, pushing my way past Nina, deliberately stepping on her foot.

"Bitch! You better watch it!" Nina said as she sat down on the couch and grabbed her foot. I took Delaney by the hand and led him out of the house. Again Officer Romanowski waited until we had driven off before he followed.

"So what happened? I asked, fearing that Delaney would turn his SUV around.

"I can't believe this shit. Nothing is going the way I wanted it. You know that I really didn't have anything in that house except my stereo equipment, clothes, and other stuff. Do you know that he cleaned me out. All I had left was a few bottles of cologne and that was it. When I see that boy it's him and me, and ain't no damn police officer in this world goin' be able to stop me," Delaney said as he gripped the steering wheel.

"I know that you don't want to hear this right now but let it go. It's not worth it. All those items are material. We can always replace everything. If you're really serious about getting your stuff back then take him to small claims court," I said calmly.

Delaney stared at me blankly and for a moment I thought we were going to have an accident. He returned his eyes to the road. "Taylor, I don't have much in this world and the few things I have mean a lot to me. Where the hell am I supposed to go from here? I only have but one person that I can count on up here, and that's you. I don't have anything to offer you. I mean I have a few dollars in the bank, but that money is tied up in CDs and investments. I want to buy a house of my own, but I won't be able to touch that money for another four months. What kind of man am I that I can't even offer my woman anything?" Delaney said as tears formed in his eyes.

I began to smile. If it weren't for Delaney driving I probably would have hugged him tightly and not let go. Instead I chose my next words carefully. "Why do men have to always be the ones who are the providers and the leaders? Here you have a woman and a man, both of whom are grown. One has fallen on hard times and the other is in a position to help. Hearing that I'm your woman delights but surprises me and we can talk about that later. But the topic at hand is friendship. It doesn't matter that I met you only a short time ago. If we're friends then that's that. Now I don't want to hear this crap again about what kind of man would you be to me because so far I'm not complaining. You have been nothing but a gentleman to me and if you don't seem to remember, you were there for me when I needed you the most, plus family is a little on the scarce side now and you're about the closest thing I've got to that right now. So just be quiet and accept my friendship with no strings attached," I said as I sat back and closed my eyes.

Enough said, I thought. Delaney and I didn't say anything else on our way home.

When we got in the house Delaney took the few belongings that he retrieved from Braxton's and I stayed downstairs and made a cup of tea. After a few minutes Delaney entered the kitchen and just stood in the doorway, staring at me. It was like he was a thousand miles away.

Only Fools Gamble Twice

"I thought about what you said, and I just want to tell you that I'm scared. I want to stay here so badly although I could find a place to rent for the time being, but you make me feel so comfortable. I've never been with a woman like you who would open up her heart so quickly, without any hesitation. It's just hard for me to trust you and then if you decide I have to go then what?" Delaney asked as he searched my eyes.

"I don't know what else to say. I know that you're scared, but then again, who isn't? Don't you think that I'm scared too? I've never been in a situation like this before. I've never even been with a *real* man before," I said as Delaney looked puzzled. "I mean I've been with guys before but never with a real man. You're grown up and strong and you signify everything adulthood is supposed to be. You're not the only one who has something to lose. The only thing we can do is put faith in God and ourselves that we're making the right decisions," I said softly before I sipped on my tea. "It's like gambling. You gotta play to win."

"Yeah, but didn't you ever hear the phrase, only fools gamble twice?" Delaney asked.

"It's funny that you say that, because I said that to my mom today."

"You didn't tell me you spoke to your mother today. How did that turn out?"

"Not good at all. But we can talk about that later. Let me ask you this, if you gamble twice and let's say you win, are you still a fool?" I responded.

"I see your point. The way I see it is that there are no easy answers, no right or wrong. I guess I have to follow my heart and see where it leads me," he said as he took my empty cup of tea and placed it in the sink.

"You're something else, Taylor Chavers," Delaney said as he placed his arms around my shoulders and gently massaged them.

12/MORGAN

When I returned to the office, Henrietta told me that Bernie had come by while I was out to lunch.

"He told me to tell you to make sure you checked your voice mail before you did anything," Henrietta said as she handed me a client's folder.

When I sat down at my desk, I smiled to myself as I noticed that the work flow was steadily going down. *Henrietta and I make a great team,* I thought. I had four messages on my voice mail. One from my dad, telling me that my mom was being released from the hospital. The doctors said she was doing remarkably well. Come to find out it was ovarian cancer, but the doctors believed they kept it from spreading. My dad was sounding like himself again. The next message was from Mister. He wanted to know what time I was getting off and what I was cooking for dinner. The third message was from a client whose folder was laying on my desk and the fourth message was from Bernie.

"Hi, Morgan. This is Bernie, I just wanted to let you know that it's official. As of today Beckerman and Leechum has acquired Remny Pharmaceuticals. Maybe now we'll be able to see the sunlight. Listen. Great job. I'll see you next week. I'm going on a much-deserved vacation. Have fun in Cancun. Take care and thanks for everything. I'll see you when I get back."

Everything was going smoothly. Now that my mom was doing better I felt much more comfortable about going on that trip with Mister. I couldn't think of a better time to take advantage of his changing ways. I immediately called him to see how things were going.

"Hey, you. You busy?" I asked when Mister's voice came on the phone line.

"Never too busy to talk to you. You sound like you're in a good mood."

"Yeah. My dad just called to let me know they're releasing my mom from the hospital this afternoon."

"Wonderful! I'm just happy that your mom is feeling much better."

"Me too. Now I don't have to worry as much about our trip."

"Don't worry. I'm going to take very good care of you when we're away. It's all about you."

"Oh, really."

"Yes, really. We *are* going to get back together. So you might as well tell all of those dudes calling your house to get ready to step off."

"What makes you so sure of yourself?"

"Because I love you. Can those jokers say the same." You're mine and I'm going to spend the whole time on our trip proving myself to you. Watch."

"Anyway, I've got to go. I'll holla at you later."

"Wait, what are you cooking for dinner? Can a brother get a meal?"

"I'm probably going over to my parents' house, so no, a brother can't get a meal. Peace," I said before I hung up the phone.

I called my client back, told him I would be off for a few days the following week and then called Collin. He wasn't there so I left him a message, telling him my mother was doing much better and that I'd talk to him when I got back from a much-needed and deserved vacation.

After I got off the phone, I called Henrietta into my cubicle and told her about the takeover and she seemed really excited. I told her that I would be taking a few days off and leaving early.

"Oh, Morgan, I'm so glad you decided to take some time off. You work way too much. Like I tell my kids, if you're going to work hard, play harder. Don't worry about a thing while you're away," Henrietta said as she grabbed my hand and gave it a squeeze.

I genuinely felt that Henrietta was a good person and as we continued to talk about family, I almost felt like I wanted to tell her about my mother's illness, but I didn't want to relive all of that again.

When I arrived at my parents' home that evening my mother was laying on the couch watching television in the living room.

"Hi, Mom. How are you feeling?" I asked as I bent down to kiss her cheek.

"Hey, pumpkin. I don't feel too bad. I'm slowly getting back in the swing of things," Mom said with a smile. "Your dad went to the pharmacy to pick up my medication. You hungry? There's lunch meat and some tuna your dad made earlier." Mom picked up the remote to change the channel.

"No, I'm cool. I had a big lunch today. I'm still full from earlier," I said, rubbing my stomach.

"How's your friend Taylor doing? The next time you talk to her tell her I asked for her," Mom said.

"To be honest, we've been passing each other in the night. I spoke to her last week and I told her that we needed to get together, but we've both been so busy. I guess she's doing fine, if not, I would have heard about it by now. You know Taylor's a drama queen," I said. "Oh yeah, did Dad talk to you about Mister and me going away to Cancun this weekend? That's if you're sure you're feeling okay," I said as I carefully looked at my mom.

"Pumpkin, I'm fine. Your father told me and I think you ought to go. You work way too hard. Just like your father. You and Mister go on and have a nice time. How many ways do I have to tell you I'm fine? Now if you don't mind, you need to go home and probably start packing. I need some peace and quiet. *Oprah* is about to come on.

"You're never going to change, are you? Nobody better bother you while *Oprah*'s on," I said standing to kiss my mother on the forehead. "I've gotta pick some things up from the mall anyway. I'll call you tonight. Tell Daddy I said hello," I said as I headed for the door.

When I got outside my father was pulling up into the driveway.

"Hey, Daddy. I was just on my way to the mall. Your wife kicked me out," I said, leaning over in the car to kiss him.

"She must be watching that tube. I guess she really is feeling better," he said as he reached in the back to grab the shopping bags. "What are you off to the mall to get?"

"I just told Mom, Mister and I decided to go to Cancun after all, *essae*," I said, in my best Mexican accent.

"Great. I'm glad you decided to go. Sounds nice. Maybe when your mom is feeling a little better, I'll take her on a cruise or something. You have enough money and everything?" Dad asked, digging into his pocket.

"Daddy, I'm fine. I got this," I said as I grabbed his arm to keep it in his pocket.

"Oh yeah, I forgot you're independent. You weren't singing that song last year when you got that car though," Daddy said jokingly.

"I let you buy the car for my birthday. I know you still want to think of me as Daddy's little girl so I let you think I was still dependent on you," I said as I climbed into the driver's seat. "I'll call you two lovebirds later on. Love ya," I said as Dad walked in the house and I drove off to the mall.

Before I headed home, I called Mister from my cell phone. He told me he had fixed dinner and that I was welcome to join him. Again, he caught me in a precarious position because I was hungry. Although Mister and I were spending a lot of time together, I wasn't quite sure that I was ready to give up the life that I had built since we had broken up. By the same token, I was extremely tired of the dating scene and Mister and I had history. I decided right then and there that I was going to give Mister another chance, and put my boxing gloves down for a minute. When I arrived, Mister was in his living room working out.

"Hey, baby. Where have you been? I thought you said you weren't going to be long," Mister said between push-ups.

"They had a huge sale at the mall so I went crazy. I even brought you some shorts and sandals for our trip. I can't wait. I'm so excited. We're going to have so much fun. Look at the bikini I brought," I said as I searched through the many bags for the bikini that I purchased. When I found what I was searching for, I held up the neon yellow string bikini and Mister raised both eyebrows.

"Where's the rest of it?"

"What do you mean? It's right here."

"No, that thing could qualify as dental floss."

"No, it's called looking sexy."

"Baby, you can wear a wool turtleneck on the beach and you're going to look good."

"Thanks, but I'll take this bikini to help out if you don't mind."

"Suit yourself. I'm just trying to tell you that you look good already."

"Thanks. I wonder if you'll still be singing that same tune when I go topless on the beach."

"What? You would do that?"

"Damn right. When in Rome do as the Romans do."

"I can't believe you would do that, but I'd still prefer if you took another bathing suit. One that's not as revealing."

"Alright. If you want, I can go to the Family Dollar store. They had a bathing suit that came down to my ankles and it had large pink flowers on it," I said, stuffing the bikini back in the bag.

"Okay. Take the bikini. It looks nice," Mister said.

"Oh, just nice. That's not the response I was looking for," I said and teasingly pouted.

"Why don't you try it on for me? I'm not feeling the full effect," Mister said as he completed his push-ups and began his stomach crunches.

"Alright. How about I let you finish your workout and I'll

be right back," I said as I gathered my bags and went into the bedroom.

"What exactly did you make for dinner?" I hollered from the bedroom.

"I made some turkey chops, stuffing, and broccoli."

I took a quick shower. I knew when Mister worked out he didn't like to be disturbed.

When I returned, Mister was still doing his sit-ups and since his eyes were closed he didn't notice me. I cleared my throat and when he opened his eyes he just stared with a blank look on his face.

"Well? Are you going to say something or not? What do you think?" I asked, spinning.

"Woman, come here right now!" Mister demanded.

I thought he was still agitated about our debate over the bikini.

"What? What's wrong?" I asked, becoming irritated. I slowly took the four steps over to Mister, not up for an argument.

If he felt that way about the bikini, I would just pack my stuff up and leave, but not before dinner. I was starving. When I reached him he grabbed my hand and pulled me onto his lap.

"I don't know if I feel comfortable with you wearing this thing. I mean I know that I can brawl with the best of them but you're trying to have me kill somebody or something. Naw seriously, you look good, baby. I can't wait. We're going to have a good time. I can't wait until we walk on the beach. I'm gon' make you look good. With my stunning looks and everything," Mister teased.

"Wake up, big man. You mean that the other way around. I make you look good," I said, mocking him.

"Okay, we both look good. Now come show Hector mon' how you American girls work it in d'states," Mister said in a terrible Mexican accent.

I didn't know what to do next. I knew this moment would come soon enough. The last time Mister and I had any dealings, I was completely drunk and this time I was sober as a judge. I knew when we got to Mexico we'd have to deal with this issue, but now it was so in my face. Mister did look and feel good and it had been a while since I had gotten my groove on.

Oh, well. We're both adults and we could handle this situation. For now, I was just going to go with the flow and see where it left me. I'd worry about other things later on.

That night, we made love over and over, and for a minute, I allowed myself to forget about all of the hurt I'd been feeling, especially toward Mister. I thought of all of the good times we shared and didn't even entertain anything other than that moment. Mister and I called in from work on Thursday so we could pack for our trip, which was the following day. We spent the entire day washing, drying, and folding his clothes, cleaning up his apartment and then we went over to my house and did the same thing over there. That evening, after we completed all of our chores, I wanted to go my parents' house before we left for our trip, just to make sure everything was in order. My dad wasn't there. He had gone to the office that evening to check on things since he hadn't been in all week. My mother told us that the following Monday my dad was planning to return to work. My mother had decided she would go back to work at the beginning of August or the middle of September, if her recovery allowed her to do so.

Mister and I stayed at my parents' home until my dad

Only Fools Gamble Twice

returned around ten and my dad agreed to take Mister and me to the airport the following morning at seven.

The morning of our trip I got up around 4:30 and fixed us some breakfast sandwiches for our plane ride. I wanted to get to the airport early because of all of the new security restrictions. Mister and I both didn't particularly care for airplane food, we figured that we probably wouldn't eat again until we arrived in Cancun.

We got to my parents' home at 5:30 and my dad said that he had already been up. He has always been the type to sleep for only a few hours. My mom was up, too, so we said our farewells and she told me not to worry, but to have a good time for her too.

When we arrived at the airport my dad double parked, took out our luggage and made sure we were checked in with the skycap before he gave me a hug, and Mister a powerful handshake, warning him to take care of his baby, and then pulled off.

As we boarded the plane, I began to get nervous, partly because I was excited about getting to Cancun and partly about the anxiety about flying after September 11.

The flight was uneventful and when we landed in Cancun, it was a hot and humid one hundred degrees, at just 11:00 A.M. I immediately took off my blouse since I had on a bikini top and lucky for Mister he had on a tank top.

"What hotel you goin' to?" a short Mexican man asked as we stood outside waiting for the shuttle bus.

"Oh, we're waiting for the shuttle. We don't need a taxi," I said, looking down at the short taxi driver.

"Sir, what hotel you goin' to?" the taxi driver asked, as

he looked to Mister.

"It's cool, man. We're waiting for the shuttle bus. We don't need a cab," Mister said as he wiped the sweat now forming on his forehead.

"There ain't no shuttles. You have to take a cab. Dat's why me asked you," the taxi driver said.

"Are you sure? I thought..." I began, as the man muttered something, waved his hand at me and then walked away.

"Excuse me," I said as I looked at the man, then Mister. We decided that we would wait and see for ourselves. After a few minutes we waited and as the crowd of travelers started to disburse, we quickly flagged down a cab. As we climbed into the taxi cab station wagon, I began to back out.

"What are you doing?" Mister asked, becoming slightly irritated as he followed closely behind.

"There are already passengers in the back," I said as I turned to look up at Mister.

"What are you doing? Get in, get in!" the new taxi cab driver yelled in his thick accent. "I thought you wanted to go to your hotel," he said again with a confused look on his face.

"There are people already in the cab, man," Mister replied impatiently.

"Get in, get in. I take all you to d' hotel," the taxi driver shouted.

"Go ahead, baby. Just get in. At this point I just want to get to the hotel and cool off. It's hotter than hell out here."

We climbed in the front seat of the taxi, me in the middle squeezed by Mister and the driver.

Only Fools Gamble Twice

When we reached the Moon Palace hotel and resort I thought Mister would flip his lid. The desk clerk informed us that we would have to wait until about four or five before we could check in. Apparently they had overbooked and were asking guests to stay at their sister hotel across town or they would simply refund any guests' money so they could stay at another hotel. It was a beautiful five-star hotel. We both agreed that we would just wait it out and they would eventually have to find us a room. We decided to change clothes in the guest locker room and do a little shopping at the mall, which was located downtown.

Mister and I shared a lot in common and shopping was one thing. We bought everything including briefcases, jewelry, shoes, and clothes. By the time we got back to the hotel, our room was ready and our bags had been delivered. The room was everything that I had dreamed it would be and because of the inconvenience, the hotel manager sent a bottle of champagne to us, which was chilling in an ice bucket by the huge king-sized bed. We quickly took showers and contemplated changing into our evening clothes. Every shop keeper that we met told us about a place nearby called Captain Kinny's, a very popular reggae club. It was the hot spot in Cancun and Mister and I both wanted to put our thang down.

"We got time for me to get some?" I asked as I stepped out of the shower, dripping on the tiled floor. I was going to completely enjoy this trip and was going to take advantage of *everything* it had to offer. Mister was getting ready to get dressed, only wearing his boxers.

"Since when have you known me to tell you no when it comes to that?" Mister asked as he quickly began to undress.

When we finally arrived at Captain Kinny's it was about eleven. Mister and I had spent more time than we had anticipated breaking in Cancun, so by the time we arrived, things was in full swing. The deejay was simply awesome. Mister and I both loved reggae music. We danced throughout the night, met other people, and drank. I couldn't help but think of how much I really missed Mister and how if we really tried, yet another time, we could be such a dynamic couple. I was also having the time of my life.

Throughout the week, Mister and I stayed in the pool, the sauna, and Captain Kinny's. The vacation was just what the doctor ordered and Mister and I made plans to come back one day.

Monday night came way too soon. We decided to just chill at the hotel restaurant and see the nightly show. Since we had been there, we hadn't really spent much time in the evenings at the hotel. The show was filled with a lot of singers and dancers and they really got the audience involved. You should have seen all of the hotel guests attempting to sing and dance the way the professionals were doing. Mister and I stood, clapped, and even tried to show the professionals how it should be done. We had a ball!

Just as the show was ending, one of the dancers did a back flip and ended up right in front of our table. The dancer went straight into a split and placed a silver tray with a lid on top of our table. I thought it was some kind of delicious food underneath. The dancer motioned for me to take the lid off and when I did, there was a rose on the tray. I picked up the rose and noticed it had the most beautiful ring tied to it. I looked at Mister who was beaming like he had just won a million dollars.

Mister went down on one knee and the whole place became extremely quiet.

"Morgan, I know we've been through so many tough times, but I love you and would be honored if you would become my wife."

I didn't know what to say. I was speechless and not to mention, what seemed like all of the hotel guests were waiting for me to say yes.

I don't know what to say." Seriously I didn't.

It seemed like my whole life flashed before my eyes and I quickly tried to think of the pros and cons. On one hand, I wasn't getting any younger. But that's not a reason to get married. You should truly want to spend the rest of your life with that person. I did love Mister, despite our past, and I knew him and he knew me. We had a history together and aside from that, I really felt that he had my back. The cons, well our past, but then isn't that why they call it a past? Don't we all deserve a second chance? I was contemplating all of this and then I realized everyone was still waiting for an answer.

"Babe, I'm waiting for an answer down here," Mister pleaded.

Before I knew it, the words were pouring from my lips. "Yes, yes, I'll marry you," I yelled loudly so everyone could hear.

Mister removed the string from the rose and placed the ring on my finger. It was truly the bomb, all three carats of it! The party was on after that. The champagne flowed all night and we partied along with the other hotel guests like it was the end of the century. I had such a wonderful time I never wanted our vacation to end.

The next morning, when we checked out of the hotel, the manager arranged for a limousine ride for us to the airport. We both agreed that it was such a kind gesture so we promised that we would spend our honeymoon at the same hotel. Our flight went off without a hitch and the lunch was even good. Everything was going so well, and the thought of me now being engaged was really getting me excited. When we arrived to Philadelphia International Airport my happiness quickly dissolved when I called my parents' home for my dad to pick us up. My sister answered the phone again and I knew instantly that something was terribly wrong.

"Mom's condition took a turn for the worse. Dad rushed her to the hospital on Sunday evening. I was waiting here for you to call. Harold is on his way to the airport to pick you guys up. I'll see you at the hospital," my sister said, her voice cracking.

"Jewel, is she all right?" I asked, fearing the answer my sister would give me.

"All we can do is pray. I'll see you at the hospital," she said, crying. I said a quick prayer and then turned to Mister.

"Your mom?" he asked quietly as I buried my head in his chest, never wanting to look at the world again.

"They rushed her back to the hospital over the weekend. I don't think it looks good. Come on, let's get out of here. Harold is picking us up," I said as I reached down to pick up my luggage.

"Wait a minute, Morgan. Now your mom is a strong woman and a fighter. She's going to be fine," Mister said as he grabbed my chin, forcing me to smile.

When we left the terminal Harold beeped his horn and waved us over to my dad's Town Car.

"We gotta stop meeting like this, Harold," I said as I climbed in the front seat.

"What's going on? How was the trip? You two look like you had too much sun," Harold said as he pulled out of the parking space and headed for I-95 South.

"How's Mom really doing, Harold? Jewel didn't say much on the phone. What's the deal?"

"They think she may have some internal bleeding. Don't worry, they're doing everything they can. She'll be okay. We've just got to keep it together and ask God for guidance."

"How's Dad? I know he must be a wreck. I knew we should have waited. Here, for the second time I'm off doing goodness knows what and my mom needs me more now than ever," I stated as I began to cry uncontrollably.

"Come on, babe. Don't do this to yourself. Your mom was fine before we left. You can't start blaming yourself. Like Harold said, the doctors are doing the best they can. Let's just be strong. Keep it together," Mister stated, placing his hand on my shoulder.

"I think now is a good time to say a prayer." Harold led us in prayer and I vowed right then and there that if God would only let my mother come out of this thing alive and well, I was going back to church.

We continued to pray and hope for Mom's recovery as we drove over to the hospital. Harold pulled up to the hospital's entrance and I got out and he and Mister went to park the car in the garage.

"I'll see you up there, baby. Don't forget to be strong," Mister stated. I faked a quick smile, and then ran up to the receptionist at the main desk. There was a heavy-set woman on the phone. I waited anxiously for a few minutes, before I noticed that she was taking a personal call. Finally after I couldn't wait any longer I exploded. "If you don't mind I'd like some fucking assistance," I said nastily. The woman peered at me over her eyeglasses and kept on talking. "Listen, bitch. My mother is in this hospital and if you don't get your fat, McNasty ass off that phone, I'm gon' rip it from your damn earlobe. Do I make myself clear?" I said through clenched teeth.

All of a sudden I heard a familiar voice call my name.

"Morgan Watson? Is that you?" I turned around to see my assistant Henrietta.

"Henrietta, what are you doing here?" I asked.

"I volunteer here on the weekends. I thought I saw you from up the hallway. What are you doing here? Aren't you supposed to be on vacation?" Henrietta asked as she looked at me, puzzled.

"I am. I mean I was on vacation but my mom--" I started but my eyes filled up and I began crying.

"Here, come over here and sit down. Do you want something to drink?" Henrietta asked as she guided me to the lobby's waiting room.

"I don't need anything to drink. I just need to find out where they're keeping my mom. The woman on the phone...I need to find my mom!" I exploded as the tears continued to fall and I tried to explain to Henrietta.

"What's your mother's name?"

"Florence Watson. She was brought in Sunday evening."

"Wait right here. I'll find out where your mom is and we'll take care of everything."

Within seconds, Henrietta had returned and was taking me to my mother's room.

On the way I explained how my mother was diagnosed with ovarian cancer and how she had surgery the previous week and was now back with internal bleeding. Henrietta told me not to worry, and that everything would be all right.

"I'll pray for you. Put it in the Lord's hands. He doesn't put anything on you that you can't handle," Henrietta said. Under normal circumstances I would have probably snapped, and asked her what the hell did she know. But surprisingly her kind words made me feel a little better.

When I arrived on the third floor, Henrietta took me to the intensive care unit's waiting room and I saw my father and sister standing there talking to the doctor who had performed my mother's operation.

"Hey, Dad, Jewel. What's going on?" I said as I looked at my dad and then my sister. My dad gave me a weak smile and grabbed my hand. The doctor laid a hand on my dad's shoulder, then walked away.

"What? Can we see Mom?" I asked.

"She's still recovering. I think we need to brace ourselves. It doesn't look good," Jewel explained.

I looked to my father to tell me this was all a big mistake and to tell Jewel to shut the hell up because she didn't know what she was talking about.

I've seen my father worried a few times in his life, but I've never seen him break down the way he did at that very moment. Thankfully, Mister and Harold came walking up and were there to hold up my dad. He had broken down to the point where he could no longer stand.

"Jewel, what? Mommy's going to get better, right?" I asked, searching for something positive in her eyes that would tell me what I wanted to hear.

"Come on, dear. Why don't you have a seat?" Henrietta said, grabbing my shoulder. I'll tell you, I almost snapped for a second but I just wiggled free and demanded that Jewel or my dad tell me something. Anything.

The doctor walked up again.

"We're moving Mrs. Watson to the recovery room. You all can visit with her in a few minutes."

When it was time for us to visit with Mom, the doctor instructed us that we only had a few minutes each. Jewel and Harold visited first. After two minutes, Jewel came out crying hysterically and Harold led her down the hall. I was still in shock. I couldn't quite comprehend why Jewel was acting so foolishly. Mom was going to be okay. I just knew it.

It was my turn to visit Mom next and I was scared stiff. I walked in slowly and almost lost my balance. My mother, the woman who had carried me for nine months, the woman who had undergone twenty-two hours of labor to bring me into this world, the woman who always looked so beautiful, was someone I didn't recognize. My mother's normal copper-brown skin looked ashy and pale. She didn't have that glow that she always had. Just as I was about to turn and run away, I saw a sparkle of light in my mother's eyes. Although her body had practically given up, her eyes still looked the same. My mother used her limp hand to motion for me. She could barely speak and she looked so frail.

"What's this?" my mother whispered as she motioned for my left hand.

"Oh, Mom, not now," I began as my mother waved me to

shut up.

"I just want to tell you to marry that man. I don't want to have to be worrying about you. Mister's a good man," my mother whispered.

"Mom, I love you so much. Please get better real soon. Don't leave me."

My mother closed her eyes and a single tear escaped her right eye. I bent down to kiss her tear away and then my father opened the door and walked in. Before I left, my mother squeezed my hand, opened her eyes, and I noticed they smiled at me. It gave me some comfort, but not the kind that I wanted. I just wanted my mother back.

The doctors told us that all we could do was wait and see how things turned out. He also cautioned us to look to a higher faith for some serious results. The doctor finally went in and told my dad he had to leave so my mother could get some rest. We all decided to head home, but my father was adamant about staying right there in that hospital. We all stayed in the waiting room all night, including Henrietta who never left me. Mister was on the left side and Henrietta on the right.

When things finally calmed down, my father surprised us all by speaking. "Your mother says we have a wedding to plan this time next year."

"Daddy, what are you talking about?" Jewel asked.

"This," I said, holding up my ring finger.

"Girl! When did this happen? my sister asked.

"When we were in Cancun," Mister responded for me. I just wasn't in the mood to be in a whole bunch of conversation. My dad stood and walked over to me slowly.

"I'm happy for you, baby. You better take damn good care of my baby like we discussed, Mister," he stated boldly, eyeballing Mister.

"Most definitely, Mr. Watson. Like I told you last week, I love Morgan and I'll spend the rest of my life proving that to her. I love her with all of my heart."

"I know you do, son. I know you do," my dad said sadly as he turned back and returned to his seat.

13/TAYLOR

On Friday, Delaney finally decided to head into his office. It had been about three weeks since he had actually stepped foot in it, but as I was recently learning, that's what consultants can actually do for a living.

Earlier in the week, I had actually landed two clients that I had been working with at my former employee's company. I was getting bored so I decided to call Morgan. It had been way too long since I had actually spoken to that child. She didn't even know that Delaney and I were sort of living together. I wondered how badly she was going to curse me out. Every time I called her at home she wasn't there. Not really strange for her because the girl is always on the go, always traveling to some exotic city on business, but she always managed to have a ball doing so. I called her office and was pleasantly surprised that she answered on the second ring.

"Morgan Watson speaking. How may I help you?"

"Well I'll be damned. You finally answered your phone."

"Hey, girl. What's up?"

"You sound like, well excuse me for what I'm about to say but..."

"Shit," Morgan answered for me.

"Exactly."

"Girl, I have been going through it."

"What's wrong? Mister?"

"No, that's actually going pretty good. Girl, I've got so much to tell you. What are you doing for lunch today?"

"I'm free. Why don't you come over to my house for

lunch?"

"Your house? Why not meet downtown?"

"I'm working from home now."

"What?"

"Yeah, I've also got a lot to tell you."

"Uh, okay. I'll be over at 12:30."

"See you then."

I jumped up and decided what to fix for lunch. I looked in the fridge and noticed I had some chicken breast thawing for that evening's dinner. I figured I would just cook everything then and that would save me some steps later.

I looked around my town house and Delaney's boxes were stacked neatly in the corner. Besides that, everything was clean as a whistle. That was the good part about Delaney and me, we both kept a clean house.

Morgan arrived around 12:30 and I was just putting the finishing touches on the grilled chicken.

"Hey, girl. Good to see you. I haven't seen you in a month of Sundays," I said as I reached to give Morgan a hug.

"Girl, I needed that hug. What's with all of the boxes in the living room?. You planning on moving or something?"

"They're Delaney's, long story. I haven't spoken to you in so long, that I don't even know where to begin. But first, what's going on? You don't look so good. Have you lost weight?" I asked, noticing my friend looked a little on the frail side.

"Yeah, I've been stressing like crazy. My mom's been in and out of the hospital these last two weeks."

"Is she all right?"

"She's not doing so good. She has ovarian cancer and Sunday, after we came back from our trip, my dad had to rush her to the hospital," Morgan explained sadly.

"Oh, my God. I'm so sorry to hear about your mom. I'm going to really say a prayer for her. I guess we're all going through a storm right about now. I don't think I know a person alive that isn't going through some sort of turmoil."

As I prepared our plates of grilled chicken breast and tossed salad, Morgan filled me in on her mother's health and all about her and Mister's trip. That seemed to bring a smile to her face when she talked about Mister.

"Look," Morgan said as she held out her hand.

"Oh, my goodness! Is this what I think it is? It's beautiful. When's the wedding?"

"Hold your horses. Yes, it is an engagement ring and we've been too busy with my mom to set a date, but I definitely want you to be my maid of honor. We'll probably set a date for this time next year."

"Girl, I'm so happy for you. You two really belong together. Mister has issues, but then don't we all. Oh yeah, I've got news for you, too, but you have to promise not to curse me out."

Just then, Delaney came in from work and the look on Morgan's face said it all.

"Hey, sweetness. Hi, Morgan. Good to see you. Sweetness, I just came home to get one of my disks and then I'm heading back to the office. I'll be home a little late," Delaney said as he planted a kiss on my forehead.

"You don't want me to make you a sandwich or anything?"

"I'm cool. I'll just grab some fruit or something. Y'all go back and do your girl talk/catching-up thang. I'll call you later," he said as he ran upstairs to get his disks and was out the door in two minutes flat.

"Okay, just what the hell is going on?" Morgan asked, looking stunned.

"Where do I begin?"

"Hold on. Let me call work and tell them I'm not coming back this afternoon. This is going to take way too long."

I filled Morgan in on the latest fight between my mother and me and how my mother refused to talk to me. Then I told her about the fight between Delaney and his roommate and how that led to him staying with me for a while, until he found a place of his own.

After we talked for a few hours, Morgan had to leave so she could get to the hospital to see her mom.

"Give your mom my love. I'm here for you, girl. You know I've got your back. We may not talk each and every day, but know that you're here," I said, pointing to my heart.

"I know," she said, giving me a hug before heading on to the hospital.

14/MORGAN

The day my mother died, just one week after my return from Cancun, I wanted to lay down and die too. I had felt pain in my life, but never like this. How could this happen? My mother was young, vibrant, full of life, and she had so much to show me, teach me. My mother would never see me get married, my children born, show me her favorite recipes.

That morning before she passed, my dad, sister, Harold, Mister and I were all in her room and surprisingly mom looked pretty good, like the color was returning to her face. The doctor had warned us, however, that Mom's condition had worsened and to prepare to say our good-byes. He allowed us all in the room, which is not hospital policy, but he understood what our family was going through, I guess.

I do feel good about one thing and that is my mom told me how fortunate she was to have me as a daughter and how proud she was of my sister and me. She told me to try to take care of my dad, check on him, and make sure he ate properly. Mom gave each us of an envelope and told us to open it when we felt we were ready. She told me that she would always be there, by my side and whenever I felt that life was getting to be too much, to call on her and she would see to it that I felt like I had a shoulder to lean on. As much as we all wanted to never leave my mother's side, we knew that her place was with her husband. I kissed her and tried to be strong as I knew she wanted me to be. I looked her directly in her eyes and said good-bye.

We sent my mother home the following Wednesday, on a rainy summer day. I hadn't figured it out yet, why all funerals seem to fall on a day full of rain. At least every funeral I've ever attended. I stayed over my parents' home the night before to help my dad and sister make the final arrangements. I knew that my dad was totally devastated, but he didn't show any sign of a beaten man. Dad wasn't his normal self, but I knew that he was putting on the best front of his life. If ever there was the picture-perfect couple, my parents were it. I had only seen my parents argue one time in my life and when they did, they kissed and made up. They were so happy together. *How could this be?* I thought as tears began to roll down my cheeks.

When we got to the church, everything was laid out beautifully. My mother was an expert when it came to floral arrangements and she loved gardening so we made sure the flowers were Mom's favorites, and ones that she would have wanted at her funeral. The service seemed to have gone too fast. Actually I couldn't tell you what happened, because when the minister began the ceremony I just blanked out. All I kept thinking about was the good times Mom and I had and how I felt that I had lost my best friend. I know Mom was the type to be many people's best friend, but all I knew was that she was mine and now I didn't have her anymore.

By the time we had gotten to the cemetery, the sun had come out and it was turning out to be a hot and humid day. Since I love the hot weather, the sun made me feel good. I closed my eyes and allowed the sunrays to beam on my face as the tears continuously rolled down my cheeks. Dad said that the it was shining bright outside because Mom's warm smile, and that we shouldn't be sad, but rejoice in her going home. I never could understand when people said that. It sounds good, but in my opinion that's bullshit. Who was supposed to feel good about their mother suddenly leaving them?

When Mister and I returned to my parents' home it was full of family and friends. I saw Taylor when I walked in. I grabbed and hugged her tightly, crying on her shoulder for what seemed like an hour. I thought that I had gotten all of my tears out, but when I saw my girl, I just let it all hang out. I felt so bad because I had ruined her silk dress, but she told me not to worry about it

"That's what friends are for. Remember what I told you the other day? I'm here for you. Don't think that you have to carry this burden alone. Turn to the Lord for your strength and know that I'm here too," Tay said as she wiped my eyes.

Delaney brought me over a plate of food and I was about to decline when I realized that I hadn't eaten in three days and that I was actually on the verge of starvation.

Henrietta came in about an hour later with a sweet potato pie and she gave me a hug and a kiss on the cheek. She told me that I was in her prayers and not to worry. "Remember what I told you. Put it in the Lord's hands and leave it there. He doesn't give us more than we can handle," she reminded me.

I didn't know what it was about this woman, but she actually made me feel a little better. Henrietta explained how she had lost her husband from this same awful disease, cancer, and that one day I would be able to face the world again.

"You never get over the pain of losing someone, but the pain doesn't hurt so badly after a while," Henrietta advised.

"But when? How long will it be?" I asked, now with tears welling up in my eyes again.

"For some people it's a month, others it's a year, and for some it's many years. The important thing is to carry the person in your heart and then move on. That's the way God wants us to live. Don't wallow in a person's home going. It's supposed to be a rejoicing," Henrietta said, patting my shoulder. "If you ever need me to talk, I'm here." She put her arm around my shoulder and gave me a hug.

Only Fools Gamble Twice

TAYLOR'S EPILOGUE

A year had passed since Delaney had moved out and bought his own townhouse. He purchased a three-bedroom place in the same development as mine. I thought it was pretty crazy, but he insisted that it was something that he needed to do for himself. We've been back to see his family again and they still adore me. Who wouldn't? Just kidding. Delaney's mom says that I'm the other daughter that she always wanted and he actually asked her, "Well will a daughter-in-law do?"

Delaney and I are still getting along just fine and we're attending church regularly. I really had a longing to get back to church and we both were finding ourselves having too many conflicts about the living-together-in-sin topic because we both wanted to take the walk together, the right way. Together we found a church home.

Last week, just before service ended the pastor asked if someone had left a package in one of the pews. Delaney stood and said, "That's mine, pastor."

Delaney went up to the altar and then grabbed the microphone. He started explaining how much his life had been changed since he had met me and then in front of everyone he got down on one knee and asked if I would marry him. Of course I said yes.

My mother and Winston are still together. So that tells you she's not doing too well. The last time I saw her was in court and she looked like pure hell. I took her to court to get legal custody of Malik. He's now living with me. I received custody of him six months ago and things are now going smoothly. The transition was a little hard at first for the both of us. You know difficulty with curfew, the phone, and girls. No one told me raising a teenager would be this difficult, but Malik is worth it. Delaney even helps me often by taking Malik out to play basketball. Delaney said that he's wants to serve as his mentor.

Of course, Winston and my mom hit the roof when they realized that I was taking them to court. They called me and cursed me out to no end, but I was ready to do battle. However, when my mom saw me in court, she actually grabbed my hand and thanked me for being there for him. How could I not be there for my family?

Tyrone finally quit his job and moved to Atlanta. My baby brother now attends Morehouse College. I've been sending him money so that he doesn't have to work. It can sometimes be too demanding to work and attend school. I want him to stay focused. My consulting business is doing extremely well, and what better way to spend my money than to invest it in one of the future leaders in our community?

Mom called me last night and told me that she wanted to break free from Winston and leave the drugs alone, but it was hard. She asked me to be patient with her. I asked if she was ready to admit herself to a rehabilitation program, but she said she wasn't sure about that. I gave her the numbers to a few programs and invited her to stay with Malik and me whenever she was ready. She told me to stop by her house so we could talk. When I got there she was high. The house looked a wreck and there were addicts everywhere. She had actually turned our place into a crack house. I couldn't believe my eyes. My mother asked me for five dollars. When I refused she cursed me out and told me to leave and never to come back. I didn't know what to do. I left and called the police from my cell phone. When the police arrived, everyone in there was arrested. I watched the officers as they handcuffed my mother and put her in the back of the police cruiser. It was the hardest thing I had to do, but I felt that it would force her to get the help she needed once and for all. God forgive me. We'll see what happens.

MORGAN'S EPILOGUE

Today, Mister and I are finally happily married and I'm starting to live again. True to his word, Mister has actually become quite the husband. Mister still continues to see Reverend Turner about his past issues. While we were in counseling he admitted that he had a lot of anger about his relationship with his father. He was abandoned by his father when he was young and that caused him to keep his feelings bottled inside. It's no excuse for his behavior, but at least he's willing to work on being a better Mister.

My dad seems to be getting by okay. Mister and I have been over to my parents' home just about every weekend to make sure that he's fine. Dad recently started his own business, a private investigation company, with one of his fraternity brothers. He said he'll probably be gone about twenty-six weeks out of the year. I think this will be good for him to get up and out of the house again.

Today was the first day that I felt like opening the letter my mom had given me on that day in the hospital. I'd like to share it with you.

Dear Morgan:

I first want to tell you that I will always love you. Since I don't believe in luck I will first explain that I'm blessed to have had you in my life. You are a beautiful, intelligent, strong, and confident black woman. When I have felt less than adequate, it was you who found a way to build me back up when life has torn me down. As my daughter you have been very supportive in everything that I have attempted to do and I more than appreciate what you have done for me.

Pumpkin, God could not be here on Earth in the flesh, so he temporarily provided us with mortals in the form of daughters, sons, best friends, husbands, mothers, and fathers. I am fortunate to have a friend in you. Know that it has been easy for me to be the mother that I am to you because of the daughter that you are to me.

I will ask God when I see Him to bless you in all that you wish to achieve. Know that everything that you hope and dream will be accomplished if you just keep Christ first in your life. He is the glue that holds us together and without Him we will just fall apart. Seek Him and you will be blessed.

I love you today, tomorrow and forever. Loving and watching over you always, Mom

Needless to say, I was a bag of water after reading her letter. As I quickly dressed for church, Mister was already downstairs growing impatient with my tardiness (that's right, I told you about that promise about one day getting back to church) I smiled inwardly and gently touched my shoulder, I knew Mom was there.

Acknowledgements

I would first like to thank God for the talent that He has bestowed upon me and for waking me up each and every day!

I wish to thank the following: Christine Green Lewis (in loving memory of) Valerie D. Lewis, my Mother, I thank you for being my best friend and confidant. I love you always! Courtney Christine Lewis Gale, mommy loves you and I dedicate my entire life to you, always. You are truly the Love of my life. I have never known love like I know in you.

My cousin and friend, Leslie Simmons, thanks for being a constant ear (you better get to reading now), Aunt Jerry Simmons, my sister, Sherilia Bradley and family, Devon, Victoria Bradley and family, Sherrie, Tray, and Kayla (Boddie) DeFederico, my favorite Aunties, Shirley A. Lewis, Brenda Lewis and Renee' Mitchell, my nephew, Anthony J. Stansbury Jr. and my niece Taylor J. Lewis (stop working your Mama's nerves☺).
My sister, Ghaka Lewis Sweet (stop working my nerves☺). I'm glad that we're working out our problems and are friends again. My girls: Rondetta and Daisa Beck, Vanita Evans (you and your family gave me ideas for another book-ya'll are crazy, but good peeps), Teresa Westbrooks (thanks to you and your family for showing me a Sista some love in Hotlanta, Bernadette and Reverend Stratton (I owe you two so much), Lourdes Marquez, Dianna Santiago (my constant ear), Diane Lauracella, Detra Duval (my Ms. Tootsie's partner), Rhonda Kennedy (my beautiful Nubian Sista), Donna Taylor (indeed you're crazy), Dianna Jefferson, Shan Ford, Michelle Jones, Beth Coleman and Geraldine Chacon; the special men of my life: Tony Baylor, Greg Wicks, Richard K. Ford, Willis (&Dawn) Richardson and Jesse Coleman. I would also like to thank Reverend Richard Worthy and his beautiful wife, Mrs. Vera Worthy. You two are the bomb and I love you!

A special thanks to my true friend, supporter, proofreader, and publicist, Mrs. Barbara Inman. Without you this book would still be on the bookshelf. You are the epitome of true friendship and I'm fortunate to have you in my life.

I would also like to thank Mrs. Barbara Lesure for proofing the reprinting of OFG2X.

Mrs. Cynthia Inman, I thank you for your friendship, encouragement and support.

Mrs. Adrianne Quarles, thanks for always being there to

listen to my complaints and most importantly my dreams. I wish you nothing but countless blessings for you and Sean (can't forget Q).

I would also like to thank Todd Inman, and Sean Quarles for being my brothers. God has a plan for everything in our lives and I know that He placed you all in my life for a reason and not a season. Words cannot begin to describe my gratitude for all that you do for me in my personal and professional life. Thanks!

Thank you to my photographer and friend, Mr. Dennis Carpenter Jones. Thank you for working with me to get this project up and running. I know that I was a pest at times, but hey, what are friends for?

A special thanks to Alison McClean and her husband Xavier. You two are wonderful. Alison, I love the website and all that you do for me.

Thanks to Ms. Laurita and Mathew. Courtney, Mom and me welcome you to the family.

To Ali Khan (Pop Pop), just continue to take care of my precious mother and God Bless you both.

I'd like to thank Ms. Joan (Aunt June), Dana, Yento (Scooter) and Kera Thompkins. How can I ever repay all of you for all that you do for me and Courtney? Thanks for taking care of my baby and for inviting us into your family.

I thank Ms. Sheria Hudson, Yanique Dailey, Pam Wise-Bowen, and Charlotte Lott. You are truly my sistas and I know that I can count on you all, always.

I can never thank you enough Mr. Travis Hunter, best selling author, *The Hearts of Men*, and *Married: But Still Looking*. What's important is that you have a gift, but you passed it on! I know you make your mother extremely proud. Without you, I would still be wandering endlessly. Thank You Much! (Give Rashaad a hug for a Sista).

I thank Eric Jerome Dickey for being a great mentor to my mentor. I wish to thank the following for going out on a limb and lending a hand: Ms. Karen E. Quinones Miller, Daaimah Poole, Todd Rose, and Dana Cobb.

Thanks and blessings to new authors, Natalie A. Darden and Alyce Thompson.

Mrs. Chandra Sparks-Taylor, I thank you for your editing services and your professionalism. I look forward to a wonderful working relationship with you. Thanks for your patience and your vision.

To the folks over at Star Shooters (my fly flyers), Stanley (Divine Designs-Buffalo), Basic Black Books (Philly), Legorious Books (Cheltenham Mall), Andre' (Ms. Tootsie's), my girl Kat, at Em Tee Coffe Cup Cafe' (Buffalo), Janice White and the special ladies of NAFE-CWO Phase II and the ladies of Delta Sigma Theta Sorrority, Inc. Thanks to James Lavar Ransome and family, Greg Singleton and Wayne Thompson for moving these books. Emerson Gale thanks for you help too.

To all of my family, friends, and my sisters, *The Charmettes, Incorporated*, thanks for listening to my undying dreams. Your kindness will never be forgotten.

A special thanks to my friend Eugenia Glenn. Thank you for your invaluable input and your gift of poetry, you have a true talent.

To all of the people who purchased the book. May we have a life-long relationship filled with great reading material between us all! For those of you that I still neglected to mention, blame it on sleep deprivation (Courtney).

Please be on the lookout for my next book, which is tentatively titled, Fate or Free Will? It's sure to be a true page turner.

                              Peace and Blessings,
                              Natosha Gale Lewis
                              An author on the move!

Please send me _____ copies of:

Only Fools Gamble Twice, a novel by Natosha Gale Lewis

I am enclosing _____ (Please add $2.00 to cover shipping and handling. No cash or C.O.D.s.)

Include recipient's address:

Name_____

Address_____
City_____ State_____ Zip_____

Email address:_____

Comments:_____

Price $15.00 USA/ $22.00 Canada   ISBN 0-9723049-0-8